NEW ENCYCLOPEDIA OF

Music

NEW ENCYCLOPEDIA OF

Music

ALAN
BLACKWOOD

WARD LOCK LIMITED · LONDON

© Text Alan Blackwood 1983

First published in Great Britain in 1983
by Ward Lock Limited, 82 Gower Street,
London WC1E 6EQ, a Pentos Company.
Previously published as Ward Lock's Encyclopedia of Music.

Text filmset in Monophoto Bembo
by Asco Trade Typesetting Ltd, Hong Kong

Printed and bound in Spain by Grijelmo S.A.

British Library Cataloguing in Publication Data

Blackwood, Alan, *1932*
   The new encyclopedia of music.
   1. Music—Dictionaries—Juvenile literature
   I. Title   II. Blackwood, Alan, *1932*. Ward Lock's
   encyclopedia of music
   780'.3'21   ML100

   ISBN 0-7063-6254-3

Frontispiece: The Wandering Musicians by C.W.E. Dietrich.

Back Cover: A young man and woman making music, a
painting by Jan Molenaer.

Contents

Introduction

Sixty or seventy years ago, an outing to a concert, the opera, or even the local dance hall was, for many people, a rare and exciting event—something to be remembered for months, even years afterwards. The only other way to hear music, unless you were very wealthy, was to make it for yourself, perhaps gathered round the parlour piano at home, or by joining in hymns at church, or just by having a good old sing-song in the pub. If you lived in a big town or city you might sometimes hear street barrel organs rattling out the popular tunes of the day.

How different the situation is now! The performance, broadcasting and recording of music is one of today's biggest industries around the world. It doesn't just involve the many thousands of musicians, orchestral players, instrumentalists, singers and rock groups who actually create music. There is the enormous production of radio and television sets, music centres, video machines, tapes, cassettes, etc., etc. and also the huge investment in new concert halls, opera houses and recording studios.

The growth of music is a marvellous thing. It has brought us music from around the world, from places as far afield and as far apart from each other as Mexico, India and Japan, and from times long past—such as the beautiful and haunting songs of medieval troubadours. Much of this wonderful music was virtually unknown until about thirty years ago. All this has, at the same time, encouraged music-making in schools, clubs and societies, on an ever-growing scale—and in this connection, the world-wide manufacture and sale of musical instruments,

including electronic equipment, is another multi-million-pound part of the music industry.

Much of this can be counted as a blessing, but the very fact that music is so easily available whenever and wherever we want it (even, sometimes, if we don't) means great music can all too easily be taken for granted. Music is often treated as little more than background noise, something we are hardly aware of any more, rather like the wallpaper in a familiar room.

The sheer variety and amount of music available has also led to a kind of fragmentation process. We only have to go into a large music store to be confronted with a bewildering display of labels or headings: 'Classical', 'Opera', 'Easy Listening', 'Musicals', 'Jazz', 'Country and Western', 'Gospel', 'Soul', 'Mainstream', 'Hard Rock', 'Acid Rock', 'Brighton Rock' and so on. We sometimes need signposts to help us find and choose what we want. But forcing music into pigeon holes—a practice increasingly adopted by radio stations around the world—creates barriers where none should exist; the only thing that really matters is whether a piece of music is good or bad.

Alan Blackwood's book clearly reflects his interest and delight in all kinds of music, right from the time of the pharaohs to the amazing sounds produced by today's electronic wizardry. He makes it equally clear that music itself cannot be apart from life. It has always existed alongside religion, politics, war, and expresses our changing attitudes and ways of life every bit as much as the clothes we wear, the machines we make, the things we say and do.

INTRODUCTION

His book is called an encyclopedia. While certainly encyclopedic in scope, it is by no means just a list of entries and subjects. The way it is organised into sections makes it much more of a true musical companion, with some parts designed to be read straight through, and others acting as a constant source of reference. I welcome, too, the range and variety of illustrations, from pictures of music in the making, to the many photographs and drawings of instruments old and new, the portrait gallery of great and famous musicians, and the carefully prepared diagrams and musical examples. It is surely a book for all music lovers.

Julian Lloyd Webber, May 1983

History

Music is a magic thing, conjured out of thin air, unseen, untouchable. It is probably too easy to come by these days; there at the flick of a switch, all day and all night long if we wish it, too readily taken for granted. In ages past the sheer effort of making music gave it real purpose and potency. In tribal societies musical instruments themselves were objects of awe and fear. They were often made from animal (including human) bone and skin, and were used to communicate with the spirit world.

Nearly all societies and civilizations have believed music to be a heavenly gift, the one sure means of contact with divine or occult powers. In India, playing sacred ragas at the wrong time of day, or wrong season of the year, was traditionally believed to destroy the power of the music and diminish or destroy the souls of performers and listeners alike. In many cultures, including Christian ones, the chanting of spells or prayers had to be done word and note perfect. If somebody made a mistake, the whole ritual had to be started again from the beginning.

In the ancient civilizations of the Middle East, people held wonderful ideas about sound and music as the power directing the sun, moon and stars in their courses—a harmony unheard by mortal ears, but sounding everywhere, holding the universe in sway. This notion of a 'Harmony of the Spheres' inspired the Greek thinker Pythagoras to make some of the first serious investigations into the mathematics of sound. By discovering the precise connection between numbers and sounds he hoped to unlock the secrets of the universe.

No one has ever proved or disproved these beautiful theories about a celestial music. Meanwhile, we have plenty of other music to be going on with, and its properties are there for all to discover.

Sound

Firstly, there is sound itself. It is a form of energy, transmitted, like most other forms of

Niccolò Paganini

9

energy, as a kind of throbbing vibration. It is feeble compared with the energy of light or electricity. It moves relatively slowly (1,222 kilometres per hour at sea level), and its strength is soon exhausted. Yet our ears are marvellously attuned to the sound energy in air. The eardrums vibrate in sympathy, and our brain interprets these vibrations as sound.

Scientists think of sound vibrations in terms of waves. The rapidity, or FREQUENCY of the wave vibrations determines the PITCH of the sound—its highness or lowness. This is easily put to the test with any odd length of string or rubber band. The tighter we stretch the string or band, the faster it vibrates, and the higher in pitch is the sound it makes. The size, or amplitude, of a sound wave determines the volume of the sound—its loudness or softness.

There is one other thing about sounds themselves that is especially important where music is

Part of the wind section of the Scout and Guide Orchestra.

concerned. This is the matter of TONE, or quality of sound. It involves the subject of HARMONICS. A vibrating string, a vibrating column of air, our own vibrating vocal cords, not only vibrate as a whole, but in parts, so that a whole series of differently pitched notes are sounding at the same time. The main, or fundamental note is the one our ears select as giving the note its pitch. But all the other pitched sounds, called overtones, are very important for the special way they 'colour' the tone of that fundamental. It is this question of harmonics that makes a note on a violin sound quite different from, say, the note on an oboe or a trumpet.

Rhythm

Among all the properties of music, after sound itself, many people would put rhythm first. Rhythms, in the sense of regulated phases of motion or action, dominate everything in the natural world—the seasons, the passage of sun, moon and tides, the progress of own lives. There may be huge cosmic rhythms spanning thousands or millions of years that we are not aware of, but that might still exercise some influence over us.

We organize the rhythms of music into so many beats to the BAR. The most common of these rhythms (which, interestingly, all fall within the normal range of the human heartbeat, from fast to slow) are of two, three or four beats to the bar. So when we speak of three beats to the bar, we mean a rhythm that goes one-two-three, one-two-three, and so on. The actual notes of the music, whether of long or short duration, fit into this pattern of beats. The basic rhythm of most rock music, or of something like a military march, in two or four beats to the bar, is usually clear enough. But even a very slow, drawn-out piece like the Prelude to Wagner's opera *Lohengrin* still has a beat to give the music a sense of pace and direction.

There are exceptions to these observations, as there are exceptions to everything. Much Oriental or Latin American music has complex rhythms, often with several patterns of beat criss-crossing each other. And not all Western

The Beatles

popular or concert music conforms to the basic types of beat described above. The well-known second movement of Tchaikovsky's *Pathétique* Symphony might at first sound like a waltz in three-beats-to-the-bar time, but in fact it has a more unusual five beats to the bar. Irregular rhythms can be very exciting. The final dance to Stravinsky's ballet *The Rite of Spring*, in which a young girl dances herself to death as a sacrifice to the gods, changes its beat from one bar to the next. But a good performance in the theatre or concert hall can have the audience on the edge of their seats.

Melody

Melodies are sequences of notes. For something to be a proper melody, these notes are not plucked out of thin air at random. They are selected from a pre-arranged sequence of pitched notes, called a SCALE. In countries like India, musicians sometimes decide on a scale just before they start to play, and the notes of their scales are often pitched more closely together than in our Western music. Many traditional folk melodies use scales consisting of five notes only—pentatonic scales (from the Greek *pente*, 'five'). Nearly all the best-loved melodies or tunes,

11

from songs and musicals, symphonies and operas, are based on the cut-and-dried system of twelve major and twelve minor scales that came into operation in European music between about 1500 and 1600.

People often talk fondly of a favourite melody flowing along, likening it to a river or stream. The nearest melody ever got to this liquid condition was in PLAINSONG or plainchant (based on the old medieval scales called MODES). Plainsong was a single line of melody, sung by an unaccompanied choir; a kind of gentle, singsong chant to the words of Latin church services. Because it followed the stress of the words it did have a flowing, meandering sound, without any clear beginning or end. Melodies, in general, are much more precisely organized, however 'flowing' and serene singers or musicians might make them sound. They mostly have an even number of bars, and a good many repeated phrases—this even balance and strong element of repetition both appeal to our basic musical instincts. Another thing most melodies have is a clear rhythm. Take away their rhythmic 'backbone' and they will fall apart.

Beyond these basic remarks, melodies vary a good deal depending upon their use to the composer. Beethoven often kept his melodies short, perhaps paring them right down to a motto theme, as in the case of the famous 'Victory-V' opening to his Fifth Symphony, because taking his musical material apart and building it up again was an important part of his method of composition. How different are the long, soaring melodies Puccini wrote to allow the characters in his operas to pour out their feelings, or a gentle, rather wistful melody like The Beatles' 'Penny Lane', which as a song is an end in itself.

The commonest criticism people make of a lot of music written this century is that it doesn't have any melodies or tunes. Composers often reply that they have tried to find new ways of creating melody, because the old rules applying to scales, rhythms, and so on, have seemed to them played out. Schoenberg went further than most in the early years of this century by inventing an entirely new kind of scale (see TWELVE-

Franz Joseph Haydn

TONE MUSIC). Sixty years later, many people are still shaking their heads over the kind of melodies he composed in this new musical 'language'.

Harmony

Harmony is the sounding together of two or more notes of different pitch. Single harmonies can be pleasing on the ear, but they are much more effective when related to other harmonies coming before and after. Real harmony is the changing relationship between notes of different pitch.

In medieval Europe, most music was composed of several interwoven lines of melody. This was POLYPHONY, and harmonies were almost a by-product of the way the composer threaded his melodies together. During Renaissance times—at about the same period that the major and minor scales were coming in—there was a gradual change from the 'many sounds' of polyphony to its musical opposite of homophony ('same' or 'single sound'). This is music consisting of a single melody supported by harmonies, often in the form of chords—comparable to a bridge supported by arches. From the time of the Renaissance, indeed, harmony has usually done much more than just support a melody. By operating according to certain rules or conventions, it can guide or steer the melody along. Even if we hear a well-known melody sung, whistled or played on its own, we are usually 'hearing' in our minds the harmonies that mark its progress. New and different harmonies can alter the character of a familiar melody just as dramatically as seeing a familiar object through the distorting effect of frosted glass.

The use of harmony, especially by such nineteenth-century composers as Liszt and Wagner, became so complex that by this century it sometimes dominated all else. Such a piece as Debussy's *Dead Leaves*, from his piano preludes, has virtually no melody, depending entirely upon harmonies to summon up its sad, chill autumn mood.

Form

Aristotle once said that a play must have a beginning, a middle and an end. This may seem obvious to us now; but somebody needed to say it, and so draw our attention to the whole question of form—every bit as important to music as to drama.

Form is the way a piece of music is organized, put together. The early jazz melodies called BLUES had a very precise form, made up of twelve bars, divided into three sections of four bars each. This $3 \times 4 = 12$ bars form of blues melody has given rise to BOOGIE, ROCK 'N ROLL, and much of today's pop music. Many other songs and dances are made up of two melodies, a verse followed by a chorus, giving us what is known as two-part, or binary form; or they have an opening tune, then a second tune, and then a return to the first, to give three-part, or ternary form.

Some of the best-known forms used in Western music are defined in the final section of this book, including CANON, FUGUE, VARIATION FORM and RONDO FORM. Perhaps most famous of all is SONATA FORM. This developed during what is called the Classical period of music (from about 1750 to 1800), when composers were inspired by the ideals of balance and proportion that mark

Johannes Brahms

many of the great buildings of Classical antiquity, such as the Parthenon in Athens. Pieces of music written in sonata form are in three linked sections, called Exposition, Development, and Recapitulation. We can liken this to a basic framework, with rhythm, melody and harmony acting as bricks and mortar. As well as being handsomely constructed, sonata form gave composers the chance to pack more ideas (including other forms like the fugue) into a single piece of music, and to invest that music with more drama, than had ever been possible before. Haydn, Mozart, Beethoven and Brahms were all masters of sonata form.

With SYMPHONIES, CONCERTOS, string quartets and SONATAS themselves (the name of a type of composition as distinct from sonata form), we are usually dealing with compositions made up of several individual pieces of music, or movements; so that the form of each movement becomes a part of the larger form of the whole work, as separate wings or halls add up to a palace.

The layout of musical scores, especially the

Louis Armstrong, Billie Holiday and Barney Bigard.

squares, rectangles and triangles sometimes used for electronic compositions, all add to this comparison between musical form and some physical plan or structure. Real music—music in performance—cannot in truth be judged like a building or a painting. We hear it as a succession of notes and chords, so that its only true dimension is time. Nevertheless, as we listen to a piece of music, we can become aware of its form, almost as though it were a visible and tangible thing.

Song

Song, using the word in its broadest sense, is the most natural, instinctive kind of music. The instrument is our own voice, something that is a part of ourselves; and in moments of great joy, sorrow or despair, we can all open our mouths and let our voices give vent to our feelings. Song has always conveyed personal feeling, or universally shared experience, more strongly and

directly than any other kind of music, indeed any other means of expression. Mothers croon to their babies in tones of love and contentment, in much the same way all over the world. Grief is another universal emotion that calls forth much the same vocal response at all times and places. There are Egyptian wall paintings depicting mourners, their arms thrown upward or bodies bent forward, as they accompany their dead pharaoh to his tomb. These same attitudes of grief, and the kind of laments that would have gone with them, can be seen and heard on our television screens as cameras follow the relatives and friends of some new victim of war or terrorist attack.

Songs are a big feature of folk music—music that is not composed by any one person but grows up with a whole race or class of people. Traditionally, no one wrote folk songs down. They were heard and remembered and passed on from one generation to the next. In the process they were constantly changing, and several versions of the same song might exist at the same time. The blues singers in the early days of jazz were folk singers. They heard each other sing the same basic refrains, which they modified on the spur of the moment to fit in with their particular mood or singing style. Blues singers were black Americans, originally slaves, or the children of slaves, and their songs nearly all conveyed their miserable plight. They often had voices cracked by years of hard living and cheap booze; but this could add true pathos to their singing. From their songs we can also learn much of the history of their time and place; of the cotton plantations, the labouring in the fields through long, hot days, the wail and rumble of the railroad trains traversing the vast American continent.

The border line between folk song and composed song is sometimes very hazy. The medieval troubadours of southern France were supposed to compose their songs. The title 'troubadour' is an old Provençal word meaning 'one who finds', in the sense of one who finds or invents his own verses and melodies. But from accounts of the troubadours, they trusted a lot to the inspiration of the moment. These minstrels had their counterparts elsewhere in Europe. In Germany there were the 'minnesingers', or 'singers of love'. Song contests were popular among them, as re-enacted in Wagner's opera *Tannhäuser*, which is named after a real medieval German minstrel knight. The Eisteddfods of Wales have kept alive such contests of song and verse, in which thoughtful composition and spontaneous fancy often go hand in hand.

The blues dwelt upon sadness and despair. The troubadours sang of love and longing. There are, of course, plenty of happy and comic songs. But it is a striking fact that over the centuries sorrow and love have been the abiding themes of so many great songs. In Renaissance times people liked to team up in groups of five or six, to sing part-songs called MADRIGALS. They did it for pure enjoyment, but most madrigals are on the subject of love, and on the sorrow of lost or unrequited love, rather than the joy of it.

The songs of the Englishman John Dowland, written at about the same time, are, on the whole, gloomier still.

In the First World War, one of the best-loved songs was 'If you were the only girl in the world'—very sad and wistful. In the Second World War, Vera Lynn became a national heroine singing 'I'll be seeing you', while German soldiers sang 'Lilli Marlene'—both equally sorrowful numbers. The great American song-writers of so many stage and film musicals—Irving Berlin, Jerome Kern, George Gershwin, and the rest—found a hundred haunting new ways of expressing both the desire and the pain of love.

Schubert was perhaps the greatest song-writer of all. He created what amounted to a new musical form with his *Lieder* (the German word for 'Songs'), writing piano accompaniments that set the scene for each song as vividly as many a stage set. He blazed the trail for a whole group or school of *Lieder* composers, including Schumann, Brahms, Wolf and Richard Strauss. Schubert certainly did write some songs of happiness and joy. But his two greatest song-cycles (groups of songs with a continuous story or theme), *The Fair Maid of the Mill* and *The*

Bob Marley

Winter's Journey, are full of sadness, ending in despair, on account of unrequited love.

This century, composers have written songs that go beyond feelings, to strike at our darkest states of mind. They have also tested the voice as never before. Schoenberg, as well as creating his twelve-tone scale, conceived a new method or style of singing, called *Sprechgesang* ('Speech-song'), in which the singer has to make the voice hover round notes rather than sustain them, as though he or she might be in a kind of delerium. He used this in his song-cycle *Pierrot Lunaire* ('Moonstruck Pierrot'), to conjure up a morbid world of dreams and nightmares. Peter Maxwell Davies wrote *Eight Songs for a Mad King*, based on words by the mentally afflicted George III, in which the performer is supposed to act out states of madness as well as sing of them.

Choirs

We think of choirs mainly in connection with religious music. Even when the music isn't strictly to do with religion, a choir can usually give it a touch of religious fervour. Listen to a group of Welshmen singing 'Land of my Fathers'. In the Middle Ages choirs were generally quite small, made up of monks quartered in their own monastery, or attached to some larger church or cathedral; and there probably was not so much fervour in their singing when dragged from their beds on some icy winter's morning to chant the day's first prayers. They originally sang plainsong (the Gregorian Chant named after Pope Gregory I is the best-known version of this); and then polyphony, which gradually developed from about 800 to 1200 AD. Polyphony, with its separate lines of melody being sung in relation to each other, needed expert singing. This reached its peak among Flemish musicians (those from what is now Belgium and northeast France). They formed what is known as the Netherlands School, and they were in demand, both for church music and sometimes to provide music at court, all over Europe.

Jacob Obrecht, Johannes Ockeghem and Josquin des Prés were three of the leading members of the Netherlands School. They often

Johann Sebastian Bach

composed their church masses and motets to very elaborate schemes, making the pitched notes of their melodies, their rhythms and phrases, all balance out like equations. They believed they were praising God by modelling their music on that marvellous mathematical and mystical idea of the 'Harmony of the Spheres'. Many churchmen, however, did not approve. In 1545, during an historic gathering of church leaders at Trent (or Trento) in north Italy, composers were told that they had become too wrapped up in their own scholarly ideas and had neglected the fact that they were supposed to be setting the words of church services to music. The audability and meaning of the words must henceforth come first. The result of these admonitions was the much clearer, purer sound we hear in the choral music of Palestrina.

By the time of the Council of Trent, the

The young Mozart, his father Leopold and his sister Maria Anna.

each occasion. Even a giant work like Bach's *St Matthew Passion*—a kind of ORATORIO based on the gospel account of Christ's arrest and crucifixion—received only one performance in his lifetime, and was not heard again for over a century, until Mendelssohn revived it. Bach's greatest contemporary, Handel, spent most of his life in England, and wrote for a more fickle public. He composed *Messiah* in less than a month (sometimes taking passages from other compositions), in his haste to get it finished while oratorio remained so popular. In the event, the first performance was a big success, George II himself rising to his feet at the stirring sound of the 'Hallelujah Chorus'.

J.S. Bach and Handel, though they cannot have realized it at the time, brought to an end a long tradition of church choral music, based largely on the methods of polyphony, stretching back four or five hundred years. From their time onward, the greatest composers are all remembered, first and foremost, for other kinds of music: opera and ballet, symphonies, concertos, string quartets and sonatas. This does not mean that composers stopped writing choral music. Haydn wrote his two oratorios, *The Seasons* and *The Creation*, also several splendid church masses, after he had finished his career as a composer of symphonies. Mozart died while working on his setting of the REQUIEM MASS. Beethoven crowned his mighty series of symphonies by adding a chorus to the finale of the ninth and last of them (henceforth known as the 'Choral' Symphony). Berlioz, Verdi, Mahler, Elgar, all gloried in the sound of a large choir.

This century composers have sometimes used a 'wordless' choir or chorus, to create a special sound effect instead of uttering the words of a text. Ravel includes a full choir like an extra group of instruments in the ravishing score he wrote for the ballet *Daphnis and Chloe*. Debussy uses a small women's chorus to create a bewitching effect in *Sirens*, the last of three orchestral pieces called *Nocturnes*. In 'Neptune, the Mystic', the last movement of his colourful orchestral suite *The Planets*, Holst also uses a women's chorus to spirit us wordlessly away to the stars.

Reformation was well under way—the rebellion against the authority of the pope that led to the foundation of the Protestant churches. Its leader, Martin Luther, wanted congregations rather than choirs to sing, and composed for them strong, simple hymn tunes, called CHORALES. J.S. Bach, who lived in the Protestant part of Germany some 150 years later, often included Lutheran chorales in his own church music. Bach was for much of his life a church choirmaster and organist, and as a regular part of his duties composed new CANTATAS for the main service on each Sunday of the year. These were usually performed once, then set aside. This practice explains why his output of music, and that of most of his contemporaries, is so large. Whether they were writing church music, instrumental pieces, or operas, they were expected to come up with something new for

Gioacchino Rossini

Hector Berlioz

Opera

Opera is a Latin word meaning 'works'; and the huge and gorgeous scale of such an opera as Verdi's *Aida*—intended to celebrate the opening of the Suez Canal in 1869—with its settings of ancient Egypt and triumphal parades, certainly is 'The Works' in every sense of the word. Opera is also more exact, and demanding, than any other kind of music on the capacities of the singers. In the realm of song men and women often perform the same songs, perhaps altering the KEY (the general pitch) of the music to suit their own voice. Not so in opera. Voices are classified according to their range of notes (their tessitura), from the highest SOPRANO, through CONTRALTO, TENOR, BARITONE, to the deepest BASS; and composers write operas with these classifications strictly in mind.

Opera did not start with all these grand designs. It began as a private entertainment among a small group of musicians and noblemen in Renaissance Italy who wanted to revive what they believed to be the true way of performing ancient Greek drama, with the lines being declaimed in a sort of sing-song voice. The man who really made something of this *dramma per musica* ('drama through music'), as it was called, was Monteverdi. He brought in instruments to accompany the action (so marking the beginnings of the orchestra as we know it), and turned the whole idea of sung or chanted drama into something really new and exciting.

Monteverdi wrote his last 'drama through music', *The Coronation of Poppaea*, in 1642. By the end of that century opera, as it was coming to be called, had mushroomed into a spectacular entertainment, and spread from its original home of Italy to other parts of Europe. It also developed two main forms: *opera seria* (serious opera), based almost entirely on stories from Classical mythology or ancient history; and *opera buffa* (comic opera), which dealt with more domestic situations, often involving foolish old men running after pretty girls. Handel wrote

Bedřich Smetana

Louis v. Beethoven.

Ludwig van Beethoven

'serious operas' for the London stage. The name for the general artistic period in which he lived was the Baroque. The buildings and paintings of the period, like those of Sir Christopher Wren and Peter Paul Rubens, were grand and opulent, and so were Handel's operas. They included an extraordinary type of singer called a castrato, a man who could sing like a boy; and this very florid kind of singing was the sensation of the age. Early productions of Handel's operas had other sensations to attract the public in what was then Europe's richest city. The first night of one of them was celebrated by the release of a flight of starlings into the auditorium.

Dr Samuel Johnson spoke disdainfully of such operas as 'an exotic and irrational entertainment'. There were composers who agreed with him. Christoph Willibald Gluck, who wrote operas mainly for the Paris stage, was anxious to sweep away the more extravagant or trivial elements of opera, and make of it something much more dignified. Mozart, at the end of the

eighteenth century, brought opera right down from the clouds and set it fair and square in the world of reality with *The Marriage of Figaro*, the first of three great operas he created with the librettist Lorenzo da Ponte. It is called a comedy, but is far more than that. Through his music, Mozart makes the characters laugh and cry, behave well or badly, like people in everyday life. At another level the opera takes a dig at the aristocracy, so giving it a sharp political edge. Mozart composed this and the more fiery, dramatic *Don Giovanni* (Don Juan) to Italian words, and in the Italian operatic style. *The Magic Flute* is a kind of German-language pantomime, but has ARIAS and choruses praising the ideals of brotherhood and the equality of man. Mozart was a musical revolutionary, just when the French Revolution was coming to the boil.

Beethoven, who grew up during the Revolution, set opera on a much weightier path. His only opera, *Fidelio*, is about a loving wife who rescues her husband from wrongful imprisonment. Through it Beethoven was expressing his own political and moral beliefs about liberty and freedom with a depth and intensity that no one had attempted before him. Wagner carried things still further. He held strong views on just about everything; politics, philosophy, religion, as well as the art of music and of opera, all of which he published in numerous books and articles. He revolutionized the form of opera itself, calling it 'music-drama', to emphasize that his work was different from everybody else's, and he filled it with his multitude of ideas. Wagner's biggest work (probably the biggest single work of art ever achieved) is *The Ring of the Nibelungs*, a colossal cycle of four music-dramas, based on Norse mythology. There are hardly any arias or melodies in a conventional sense. Instead, 'leading motives' or motto themes stand for the characters (e.g., Wotan chief of the gods, Brunnhilde his daughter, Siegfried the hero), objects and ideas (e.g., Valhalla home of the gods, the sword Nothung, magic fire). These are threaded together musically into a continuous tapestry of sound by the orchestra, against which the singers declaim their lines. Ever since its first production in 1876 at Wagner's own specially built festival theatre at Bayreuth, people have been arguing about the meaning and message of 'The Ring'. The dramatist Bernard Shaw, who was a pioneer socialist, said it was a vast fable or allegory about the evils of capitalism. Adolf Hitler took Wagner's work as an example and an inspiration for his own ideas about power and racial superiority.

Giuseppe Verdi, who lived at the same time as Wagner, became a political hero to his Italian fellow countrymen. They identified him and his operas with the movement for a united kingdom of Italy. Verdi himself, though, was not so wrapped up with theories and ideas as Wagner. He followed the Italian tradition of composers such as Donizetti, Bellini and Rossini, who glorified the human voice and gave audiences what they wanted in the way of entertainment. Verdi's achievement was to add tremendously to the musical and dramatic force

George Frideric Handel

of opera without turning it upside down. His successor, Puccini, continued the process in Italy; so in other countries did Bizet, Tchaikovsky, Mussorgsky, Smetana and Massenet.

Leaving aside huge film and television epics, opera has always been the most costly form of entertainment. It has carried with it big financial risks, and throughout its history has probably ruined far more composers, producers and sponsors than it has made rich and famous. Nevertheless, opera houses survive, people still flock to see opera, and many composers still want to write operas. One of the most successful opera composers of this century has been Britten—all the more striking since no other Englishman before him, with the exception of Purcell, had ever made his mark in the opera house. Britten's first opera was *Peter Grimes*, a grim story set in a Suffolk fishing village. *Billy Budd* is a drama set on board a warship of Nelson's day. *The Turn of the Screw* is a chilling ghost story. The style of these operas may take a bit of getting used to, but they are just as gripping as *Rigoletto* (Verdi), *Tosca* (Puccini), *Carmen* (Bizet), or any other of the world's best-loved operas.

Dancing

Dancing is to do with rhythm, that most powerful and gripping ingredient of music. We know there was dancing 30,000 years or more ago, because of the crouching, leaping figures depicted on stone carvings and paintings dating that far back in time. These dances were almost certainly to do with sympathetic magic—the belief that if you act something out you can make it really happen. Since survival in those remote times depended, above all else, on having enough to eat, and food meant hunting, dancers acted out the parts of the beasts and those who hunted them. In the magic dance the hunter killed the beast. Other ritual dances, from time immemorial, have been concerned with making it rain and making the crops grow, curing the sick, destroying enemies, pleasing or appeasing the spirits—all those unseen forces that explained the changes from darkness to light, winter to summer, birth and death, famine and plenty. They often involved elaborate make-up and costumes—thus combining what was thought of as part of the magic with the universal human delight in dressing up and putting on a show. All over the world people still enact them, the sun dances, devil dances, and the rest. Even the harmless-looking English Morris dancers, with top hats, handkerchiefs and bells on their ankles, once were concerned with the power of light over darkness, life over death. Now they're good for tourism.

Dancing, like singing, has also been one of the simple pleasures of life, because it comes so naturally. It was, for hundreds of years, a great relaxation for country people and poor town people, who made up their dances and the tunes to go with them. This folk dancing—which sometimes grew into a quite complicated performance—has always been happily accepted by people in general. Indeed, in our own times, folk songs and dances have become a matter of national pride.

Other kinds of dancing have long been viewed by some with suspicion and disapproval, because they can easily express physical attraction between men and women. Creatures like peacocks may strut about with their feathers up to attract peahens. The equivalent goings-on between humans have, for some people, always been thought of as sinful. This was the case in Renaissance times, when dancing at court became so fashionable. Most court dances were taken from the humbler dances of the peasants and turned into much more sophisticated and graceful 'measures'. Henry VIII and his daughter Elizabeth I both loved dancing. No matter; dancing soon had such a bad reputation that laws were passed against it. Dancing the stately Spanish SARABANDE was at one time punishable by two hundred lashes or banishment. The MINUET, GAVOTTE and gigue, all had a murky reputation at first. In the nineteenth century, the WALTZ, which made a fortune for the Strauss family of Vienna, was both the world's most popular dance and a matter of great scandal, since it allowed men and women to hold each other's bodies.

This century popular dances based on the rhythms of jazz and Latin American music—the CHARLESTON, TANGO, JIVE and rock 'n roll—all created a scandal in their time. Today's discotheques, with their highly amplified, thudding music and flashing lights, are attacked

Giuseppe Verdi

Children making music, a painting by Jan Molenaer.

because of the way they pulverize the senses and drive out thought and feeling. There is nothing new in this. The religious dervishes of Muslim countries, and others, have for centuries danced themselves into a state of trance, sometimes to the very point of death.

The specialized type of dancing we call BALLET began in France during the long reign of Louis XIV—which is why all the traditional ballet steps and movements have French names. Louis was known as 'The Sun King' because he built the great palace of Versailles near Paris, and attracted so many people of talent to his court; and there is a picture of him, dressed in a ballet costume representing the sun. These French opera-ballets by Lully and other composers at Louis XIV's court were extravagant but on the whole light-hearted entertainments; and for a long time ballet was not treated very seriously, at least as far as the music was concerned. Composers from the time of Lully through to Delibes (*Coppélia*) and Tchaikovsky (*Swan Lake*, *Sleeping Beauty*, *The Nutcracker*) wrote ballet music that was always easy on the ear,

knowing it was the spectacle and dancing that people came to see. In France itself, operas nearly always included a ballet sequence, and people not interested in the whole opera used to time their arrival at the theatre just to catch the ballet.

The other great home of ballet has been Russia, due to the close cultural links between France and Russia going back to the time of Peter the Great. The event that changed the face of ballet was the arrival in France, in the early years of this century, of Sergei Diaghilev's Russian Ballet company. Diaghilev commissioned from his fellow countryman Stravinsky scores to the ballets *The Firebird*, *Petrushka* and *The Rite of Spring*—the last of these so shook the audience on the opening night that there was a riot. He commissioned other brilliant scores from Debussy, Ravel and Falla. He employed the finest dancers and choreographers—the people who plan the steps and movements in a ballet—and artists such as Pablo Picasso to design stage sets and costumes. So Diaghilev's Russian Ballet made people take ballet as seriously as opera or concert music; and today ballet is as adventurous and advanced in its ideas as any other of the performing arts.

22

Instruments and Orchestras

Until this century and the invention of electronic devices, musical instruments had not changed much in thousands of years. They were constantly being modified and improved, but remained basically the same. Carvings and paintings from the ancient civilizations of Babylon, Assyria, Egypt, show us drums, xylophones, harps, flutes and trumpets, that have quite a familiar look about them. In a few cases we have recovered actual examples of ancient instruments. One such was a trumpet from the tomb of the Egyptian pharaoh Tutankhamun who died about 1340 BC. It sounds a high, clear, penetrating note, as though summoning up the long-dead pharaoh's spirit!

For much of history, as far as we can tell, instruments were used mostly to accompany singing and dancing. Through the long centuries of the European Middle Ages, troubadours and other minstrels played small, portable harps to accompany their songs; clowns and jugglers at church feast days and other holidays played a variety of drums, pipes and stringed instruments; and in church itself, choirs were sometimes accompanied by organs and bells. Soldiers and huntsmen also signalled to each other with trumpets and horns. In all these examples, the instruments took second place to some other activity.

This situation began to change with the Renaissance. This French word means 'rebirth', and refers to the reawakening of interest in the civilizations of ancient Greece and Rome that first occurred in Italy around the year 1400. In the next two hundred years it produced throughout Europe big advances in the arts, literature and philosophy, the sciences, commerce and exploration. Music in general, and musical instruments especially, benefitted from all this. Instruments themselves were better made, thanks to the inventiveness and skill of Renaissance craftsmen. Commerce and trade created more wealth and leisure (at least for some). The invention of printing made music easier to come by, and encouraged its composition. The nobility and the rising class of

Antonio Vivaldi

merchants and bankers took up music as a recreation. They liked to sing madrigals, as we have read, and they learnt to play one or more instruments. Such accomplishments were considered part of being a true Renaissance lady or gentleman. All the best households possessed a whole case or chest of instruments—viols, lutes, recorders—which might form the basis of a small band or CONSORT. It is from this time that composers began to write seriously for instruments on their own. Antonio de Cabezon in Spain and William Byrd in England composed many pieces for the keyboard virginals and harpsichord. John Dowland, renowned for his songs with lute accompaniment, wrote many pieces for the lute on its own.

A sure sign of the way the tide was flowing in favour of instrumental music was the growing fame of instrument makers themselves. During the seventeenth century, in the Italian town of Cremona, several families of craftsmen started making violins, violas and cellos—rather like streamlined versions of the older bowed stringed instruments, the viols. Their names—Stradivari, Guarneri, Amati—have long since echoed round the world, some examples of their work now virtually priceless. In Antwerp the Ruckers family was famous for its manufacture of virginals and harpsichords. In Germany, Andreas and Gottfried Silbermann became celebrated organ builders.

The new and improved instruments that these fine craftsmen produced were an inspiration to the greatest composers of the Baroque period, and in some cases led to the creation of new musical forms exclusively to do with instrumental music. A whole generation of Italian composers, notably Corelli and Vivaldi, wrote hundreds of works in the CONCERTO GROSSO style for string bands. Domenico Scarlatti composed well over 500 single-movement harpsichord sonatas which introduced many new keyboard playing techniques, and pointed the way towards the full development of sonata form. J.S. Bach, who knew the Silbermanns, wrote the greatest of all pieces for the organ in the form of PRELUDES and fugues, chorales and FANTASIAS. A rich quantity of other instrumental music flowed from Bach's pen: the 'Brandenburg Concertos', six works in concerto grosso style, that experiment with different instrumental groupings; SUITES of dances for violin and cello; more suites for the harpsichord, and a monumental group of Forty-eight Preludes and Fugues, subtitled 'For the Well-Tempered (Tuned) Keyboard', because they were prompted by a new system of tuning keyboard instruments.

Kings and princes also helped in this flowering of instrumental music. Louis XIII and Louis XIV of France both supported string ensembles, proudly called 'The King's Twenty-four Violins'. Frederick the Great of Prussia was an enthusiastic flautist and paid other gifted musicians, including J.S. Bach's son Carl Philipp Emanuel, to join his court at Potsdam, near Berlin. The orchestra at the court of Mannheim was reckoned the best in Europe in the eighteenth century. The English author and scholar Dr Charles Burney, on his travels, called it 'an army of generals', meaning that everyone in it was a top-class player. The Mannheim orchestra was directed by a succession of forward-looking composers, including Johann Stamitz, and was a showpiece for striking new orchestral effects, such as the gradual, controlled build-up of sound called a CRESCENDO.

Best-remembered of all is the court of Prince Nicholas Esterhazy of Austria-Hungary, where Haydn was for many years the musical director. With another good orchestra at his disposal, Haydn did as much as anyone to establish the brand-new type of orchestral composition called the symphony. This grew out of an earlier type of Baroque overture called SINFONIA, played by theatre orchestras to get an audience settled before the start of an opera or ballet. Haydn wrote over a hundred symphonies, shaping them into compositions of four contrasted 'movements', and perfecting the kind of orchestral balance of sound also being achieved by the Mannheim musicians. He also composed many string quartets, which describes both the ensemble itself and the type of composition—a more intimate form of the symphony.

All this new instrumental music (we are talking roughly of the period 1750–1800) is called 'Classical', largely because it shares with the buildings of Classical Greece and Rome, and all those modelled on them, the same concern for form and order. Such music is also known as ABSOLUTE MUSIC, since it is for instruments only, has no connection with words, and is therefore regarded as music pure and simple. Many of Haydn's symphonies and string quartets do have nicknames, such as the 'Surprise' Symphony, the 'Lark' String Quartet, but these generally refer to some passing feature of the music and have no real connection with it. Mozart was the other great composer of this Classical period, and of this absolute music. What strikes most listeners is the quality of deep feeling they believe they can hear in some of Mozart's symphonies, concertos, string quartets and string quintets—as though they are an echo of all the feeling and drama of his operas. Mozart, though, gave no special names to his instrumental compositions. They are beautiful purely —'absolutely'—as music.

Beethoven wrote some of the very greatest instrumental music. It is mostly in the Classical forms of symphony, concerto, string quartet and sonata; but throughout his life, Beethoven was constantly changing and enlarging these forms, and charging his music with a new intensity of feeling, as though he wanted to 'speak' through it in a very personal way. As an indication of this, he gave special titles to some of his compositions. There are the *Pathetique* (full of

Top: A student at the Royal National Institute for the Blind's Chorleywood College.
Right: Frédéric Chopin

feeling) Piano Sonata and *Appasionata*; the *Eroica* (Heroic) and *Pastoral* Symphonies. Another piano sonata has its three movements labelled 'Farewell', 'Absence' and 'Return', which refer to events in his private life. Beethoven was the great link between the Classical and Romantic periods of music.

The Romantic movement started at about the same time as the French Revolution. Personal and artistic freedom were its ideals. Romantic poets loved the open air, forests, rivers, mountains, seeing in nature the freedom they themselves desired. For them, what they wanted to express, of their thoughts and feelings, was more important than any rules or conventions about how they should express it—i.e., content was more important than form. Romantic composers viewed their art in much the same way; and while they sometimes set words to music, as songs, choral pieces or operas, they mostly continued writing for instruments as Classical composers had done before them. It was the kind of music they wrote that was so different.

Their favourite solo instrument was the piano, which had replaced the harpsichord by the end of the eighteenth century. In the next hundred years manufacturers like Erard of Paris, Broadwood of London, Steinway of New York, kept building larger, stronger, more sonorous pianos, to inspire Romantic composers. Schumann and Chopin wrote piano pieces that sound wonderfully free and spontaneous, generally preferring forms of their own creation rather than established types of composition like sonata form. Liszt—a phenomenal pianist himself—often went further, turning his piano music into pictures-in-sound of places and events.

Top left: Modest Mussorgsky
Top right: Felix Mendelssohn
Left: Part of the brass section of the Scout and Guide Orchestra.

New versions of orchestral instruments came along as well, helped by the technical advances of the Industrial Revolution. The horn, for example, was made with valves, allowing it to sound many more notes. And the orchestra was set ablaze by other Romantic composers. Berlioz treated the orchestra very like an artist applying paints to a canvas. He wrote a book on this new art of orchestration, detailing the effects of musical 'colour' to be achieved with different combinations of instrument. We can hear the results in a work like his *Fantastic* Symphony, describing the strange visions of a young man (really the composer himself) in a kind of delirium of love. Music like this, where every note, every bar, carries some special meaning, conveys some scene or action, is called PROGRAMME MUSIC. Nearly all Romantic orchestral music has a 'programme' of some kind. That of Mendelssohn's *Hebrides* Overture ('Fingal's Cave') is the sea lapping round the granite rocks of the Isle of Staffa off the west coast of Scotland. Not all music of the nineteenth century was so Romantic in mood and style. Brahms stuck closely to Classical forms with his symphonies, concertos and many instrumental compositions, and in his lifetime was a hero to those who thought the likes of Berlioz, Liszt and Wagner had taken leave of their senses. The general tendency, though, was for composers to pile on the drama, make everything blaze with 'colour', until the orchestra dominated all else. Wagner, though he wrote operas and music-dramas, was also one of the greatest orchestrators. All other famous composers towards the end of the nineteenth century—Tchaikovsky, Rimsky-Korsakov, Mahler, Richard Strauss—were masters of orchestration. Cow bells and wind machines were among the special effects they added to an already gigantic orchestra—grown from an ensemble of about thirty-five players in Haydn's day to a gathering often of over one hundred musicians.

The Romantic movement also inspired many composers to feel patriotic, at a time when the old dynasties of Europe were breaking up—due largely to the Napoleonic Wars—and new nations were emerging. Such musical patriotism was infectious, and by the early years of this century nearly every European country had composers writing in a 'nationalistic' style. This was usually based on their country's traditional folk songs and dances. Dvořák and Smetana in Bohemia, Mussorgsky, Tchaikovsky and Borodin in Russia, Grieg and Sibelius in Scandinavia, Falla in Spain, Elgar in England, all wrote works for the orchestra or piano that have the unmistakable ring of their respective homelands.

Debussy and Ravel wrote very refined and subtle music, typical of much French art and literature, though not based on French folk music. Much of it goes under the heading of 'musical impressionism', a term borrowed from the school of French impressionist painters, such as Claude Monet. Debussy in many of his compositions, for solo piano or full orchestra, suggested images of cloud, rain, wind and sunlight—subjects dear to the impressionist painters. He was one composer who had a big influence on the way instruments have been used this century. Others have been Schoenberg, on account of his twelve-tone methods of composition; Bartók, who created his style from a deep study of Hungarian and Romanian folk music; and Stravinsky, one of the leaders of the so-called Neo-Classical school, that turned its back on everything to do with Romanticism. 'The crowd expects the composer to tear out

his entrails and exhibit them!' Stravinsky said scornfully of the late Romantic music of composers like Mahler.

Jazz musicians have contributed much to instrumental music. They started by playing instruments often acquired from the old military bands of the American Civil War; and trumpets, cornets, trombones and clarinets, have remained the principal instruments of jazz bands, from their early days in New Orleans almost up to the present. The other instrument taken up by many jazzmen has been the saxophone, which was originally intended for French military bands. When white musicians became interested in jazz they introduced other instruments like violins, but by so doing turned jazz into the much silkier-sounding dance music known as SWING. One other stringed instrument, the guitar, took off on its own during the 1950s, when the jazz piano style called boogie gave rise to rock 'n roll.

Rock 'n roll guitarists mostly had electric instruments, which produced more volume and altered the tone. Their successors in the field of rock and pop rely almost entirely upon electronic instrumentation, creating sound effects that even orchestral wizards like Wagner, R. Strauss, Debussy and Ravel could not have achieved. The names of some pop and rock groups—'Tangerine Dream', 'Soft Machine'—suggest the dream-like, surrealist sounds they produce.

Many other musicians have experimented with new sounds. American composers John Cage and Henry Cowell modified the sound of pianos by tampering with the strings ('prepared pianos'), or using the flat of the hand to create 'note clusters'. Varèse used sirens in orchestral pieces, Gershwin had fun with car horns in *An American in Paris*, Luigi Nono included recorded sounds from a metal works in his piece *La Fabbrica Illuminata*. Messiaen has been attracted to one of the first completely electronic instruments, called the Ondes Martenot. Its strange, other-worldly tones fit in well with the mystical character of much of Messiaen's music. Boulez and Stockhausen—two of the big names in contemporary music—were among the first to use

Duke Ellington in rehearsal discussing a score with bass player
Ernie Shephard.

tapes, to record sounds of instruments or voices, then speed them up, slow them down, dissect and reassemble them, like fragments in some musical kaleidoscope. This *musique concrète* ('concrete music'), as it was originally called, was the start of what we might well call our own Space Age music.

Style and Interpretation

A big part of music making is to do with style and interpretation—two terms that overlap a good deal in meaning. In popular music, the style of the performer often counts for more than anything else. Many of the old music hall artists could hardly sing at all; but when some-body like Harry Champion belted out 'Boiled Beef and Carrots', he did it with such gusto that nobody cared about the tune. Super stars of the dance band and swing era—Bing Crosby, Frank Sinatra, Judy Garland, Billie Holiday—all sang the same hit songs, but each delivered the same song in his or her own special style, like dressing it up each time in a different suit of clothes. It was, as the saying goes, very much a case of 'the singer, not the song'. With rock 'n roll and the start of pop and rock music as we now think of it, style meant more still. Elvis Presley, The Beatles, Jimi Hendrix and many more stood for a whole way of life. It wasn't just the music they dressed up in new 'clothes'. The actual clothes they wore, their hair-styles, what they ate and drank, in some cases the drugs they took, were all part of their performance. Their music, and all that went with it in the name of style, helped to shape the way of life of whole generations.

Jazz and pop music instrumentalists have never held the centre of the stage to that extent, though style has been just as important to them. The way such pianists as Art Tatum, George Shearing, Erroll Garner played a tune was often more interesting than the tune itself. The same can be said of jazz saxophonists Ben Webster, Stan Getz, Coleman Hawkins, Charlie Parker; or of trumpeters, ranging from the full-blooded New Orleans style of Louis Armstrong to the cool, ethereal sound of Miles Davis.

For long periods in the history of European music, style was mainly to do with methods of composition and performance, which even the greatest musicians had to keep to. To a large extent, J.S. Bach, Couperin, Rameau, Handel, Haydn, Mozart, to name but a few, all composed music, and performed it, in accordance with the required style of their time and place. From the time of Beethoven onwards, however, when composers gained more artistic freedom, all the great and famous ones did develop styles of their own. Beethoven himself, Chopin, Berlioz, Wagner, Verdi, Tchaikovsky, Puccini, Debussy, Elgar, Sibelius, Copland, Prokofiev, Stravinsky . . . all created a sound, a style to their music as personal and distinctive as their own signature or thumb print. From about the same

Barbara Thompson playing saxophone.

Peter Tosh at a charity concert in Kingston, Jamaica.

time—the early years of the nineteenth century —there has also been a general tendency for composers to concentrate on their task of composition, leaving others—executive artists—to interpret and perform their work.

Pianists have always headed the list of solo performers, since more great music has been written for the piano than for any other single instrument. Despite what we have just said about the division between composers and executive artists, Chopin was a regular performer of his own music, public recitals doing much to weaken his already poor health and speed his death. Liszt, as we have already noted, was a phenomenal pianist, one of the first in the long line of what we call virtuoso performers—those who glory in technically very difficult, very brilliant-sounding music. Another virtuoso pianist who became a household word sixty years ago was Ignaz Paderewski. There was even a music hall song written about him. 'Down he goes on his two elbows, Bangs at the piano with the end of his nose—When Paderewski plays!' The greatest concert pianists, though, have always put the music first, thinking long and hard about the composer's intentions. Artur Schnabel, who specialized in Beethoven, expressed his sense of dedication when he said, 'great music is better than it can be played'. Another celebrated German pianist, Walter Gieseking, was one of the first to champion Debussy's music—as different as it could be in character and sound from the music of Beethoven.

All the differences in style and technique we find among pianists are equally evident among violinists, cellists and other instrumentalists. Singers, too, offer us a wide variety of interpretations of the same operatic roles or songs. Most singers specialize, some in Wagner, others finding their voices and temperaments better suited to the 'bel canto' style of Italian opera, or to the much more personal and intimate style of *Lieder* and other types of song. But the biggest names among executive artists, as you can see at a glance in any record shop or library, are those of conductors.

A participant in the Scout and Guide Folk Fest 10 at the Albert Hall.

Before the nineteenth century there were no conductors as we think of them today. To start with, it was a rare thing for a piece of orchestral or choral music to be published as a complete score, with all the parts printed together. Composers handed out separate parts to the various performers then directed the performance as best they could by sitting at a harpsichord and playing what was called the CONTINUO part— setting the tempi and guiding their colleagues through such tricky passages as a change of key. Such routine practices could not cope with concert music from the time of Beethoven onward.

Larger orchestras, increasingly original and complicated music, required someone to study the score in detail, lead the orchestra through rehearsals and conduct the players from a platform or rostrum where they could see and be seen. Mendelssohn was one of the first really professional conductors, in addition to his work as a composer. He took charge of the Leipzig Gewandhaus Orchestra, the first to be established on a modern commercial basis, paying its way with public concerts, instead of being attached to some royal court. Other nineteenth-century composers did sometimes take up the conductor's baton. Wagner, by all accounts, was a good conductor. Tchaikovsky didn't enjoy it at all, standing on the rostrum and holding his

Miles Davis on trumpet.

life—sometimes with a joyous shout. Arturo Toscanini had the reputation for scrutinizing a score down to the minutest detail, then getting the orchestra to play exactly what the composer had indicated. He could also lose his temper. There is the story that when one orchestral player annoyed him, Toscanini stopped the rehearsal, asked the unhappy musician when he had been born, then snarled in his thick Italian accent, 'Was a black day for music!'

Conductors, like other executive artists, often have their preferences for the work of one composer rather than another. Wilhelm Furtwängler and Otto Klemperer were famous for bringing out the 'architectural' qualities of the symphonies of Beethoven and Brahms. Leopold Stokowski concentrated on the quality of orchestral sound, and revelled in the rich orchestration of composers like Tchaikovsky. Conductor-composer Pierre Boulez is expert at unravelling the more puzzling aspects of the works of such composers as Schoenberg and Webern.

Some conductors enjoy working in an opera house, where the time-scale and general approach to the work is quite different from that of the concert hall. They rehearse for weeks, perhaps months, with the orchestra, singers, and producer. Once an opera production is ready, the conductor, along with the cast, will usually stick with it through a number of performances, instead of constantly moving on to new programmes, as would happen in the concert hall.

Apart from the music itself, and all the different interpretations that can be put upon it, styles of performance are changing all the time. To take the violin as a prime example, fifty or sixty years ago, violinists used to 'scoop' as they played, that is, glide up or down from one note to the next, instead of playing each note in a clear-cut manner—a mannerism we can hear on very old recordings. Further back in time, violinists and cellists did not play with the slight wobble or vibrato effect that modern players automatically bring to each sustained note. Notes were played with a flat, even tone, though perhaps with a slight increase in volume as the player drew his bow across the string. In

head with one hand, apparently scared it might fall off! By the end of the century, however, the greatest conductors were specialists in their craft; men like Hans von Bülow and Hans Richter, friends of both Wagner and Brahms, who wielded almost as much authority as the composers themselves.

The most obvious thing about conductors is their manner on the rostrum. Some wave their arms about, even stamp their feet, as though driving the orchestra on by their energy and excitement. Others move little, perhaps stand with eyes closed, appearing to direct the performance by sheer force of will. Much of their work is done at rehearsal. Recordings of Bruno Walter in rehearsal reveal him tackling virtually each bar of the music in turn, leaving nothing to chance. Sir Thomas Beecham, by contrast, often used to let the orchestra play through an entire piece, making just one or two comments in conclusion. He liked to hold something in reserve for the concert itself, relying on his flair to bring the performance spontaneously to

Top: The National Youth Orchestra of Great Britain rehearsing with conductor Riccardo Chailly.

Above: A girl on drums taking part in the Scout and Guide Orchestra course at the Royal College of Music in London.

times past there was also a good deal of trilling and other decorative finger work that was taken for granted by musicians and therefore seldom, if ever, written down. Couperin wrote a book about playing the harpsichord which now provides us with valuable information about the special way of playing and ornamenting keyboard music in early eighteenth-century France that we could never acquire simply by studying printed copies of the music.

Today there are musicians who specialize in giving what they believe to be authentic performances of old music, using instruments appropriate to the period and in accord with the playing styles and musical ornamentation we have just discussed. A famous work like Handel's *Messiah*, written nearly two hundred and fifty years ago, can quite startle listeners the first time they hear it performed, using the right kind of instruments, and singing it in the style of Handel's own time—like taking a fresh look at an old painting after layers of varnish have been removed.

The Italian dancer Carlotta Zambelli (1875–1968) in *Danses de Jadis et de Naguère* at the Paris Opera.

A German positive organ probably made by Gottfried
Fritzsche in 1627.

Musical Instruments

Sounds are combinations of pitch, volume and tone. When they are indiscriminately mixed together we call them noise. When they are acoustically fashioned and balanced we consider them as musical sounds. The musical instruments which men and women have devised to produce the desired blends of pitch, volume and tone have themselves been combinations of a few basic factors—namely, the source of sound, materials, size and shape. We may liken the factors that go to make up musical instruments, and the factors that go to make up sounds, to the two sides of an equation. Take away or add something to the structure of an instrument and we bring about a corresponding change in the nature and quality of the sound. This is the fascinating story of musical instruments and the way they are played.

Their scientific classification, using terms of Greek origin, is according to their source of sound:

Idiophones are instruments of wood or metal that vibrate within themselves when struck. Wood blocks as used in varying sizes in a xylophone, cymbals, gongs and bells are all idiophones.

Membranophones are instruments that use a stretched membrane, hide or skin as their basic source of sound. Drums are the principal types of membranophone.

Aerophones are instruments requiring a column of air to be set in motion inside a tube or pipe, usually by the player's own breath. Whistles, flutes, recorders, horns, trumpets, organs are all aerophones.

Chordophones are instruments whose source of sound is the vibration of a tightly drawn string or wire. The violin and cello, harp and guitar, piano and harpsichord are examples of chordophones. The human voice might also be considered as a chordophone, although it also needs our own breath to make it sound.

There is, however, an alternative system of classification, which divides the majority of instruments up into percussion, strings, woodwind and brass. It places such instruments as the piano and organ into the special category of keyboard instruments. This is the classification best known to music-lovers, and the one we shall follow here.

Percussion Instruments

These are instruments that are struck in some manner—drums, gongs, cymbals, bells and more local and specialized instruments such as castanets. Within this broad family of percussion instruments, the big division is between those of definite and those of indefinite pitch.

Many drums are percussion instruments of definite pitch. They have a membranous playing-surface tightly stretched over a bowl-shaped frame which acts as a resonator—i.e. it amplifies and to a certain extent modifies the sound of the vibrating membrane. Traditionally

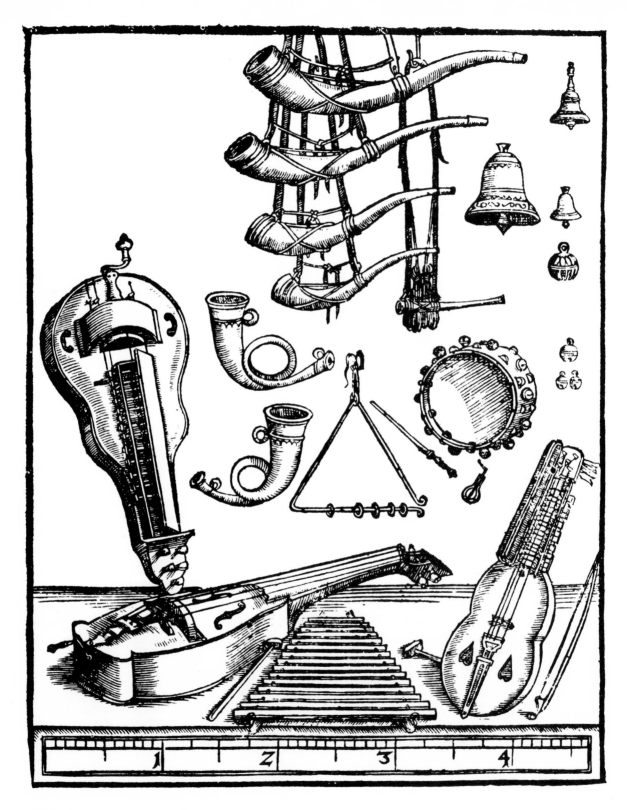

This fine old German print includes instruments belonging to
each of the four scientifically defined groups.

Opening of Beethoven's *Eroica* symphony showing how the instruments in a score are organized into woodwind, brass percussion and strings.

Traditional type of kettledrum from South India.

this membrane was made of animal hide, which in the past often included human skin; and it was a common belief that to play such a drum was to call up the spirit of the dead animal or person. The matter of pitch is determined both by the size of the drum and by the tightness of the membrane. A drum with a large playing-surface and correspondingly large resonator will produce a much deeper-pitched note than one constructed on a smaller scale. At the same time, a very tightly stretched membrane will vibrate quicker and so produce a higher-pitched note than a membrane that is comparatively slack.

In an orchestra the principal percussion instruments of definite pitch are the kettledrums, or timpani. They can be tuned by adjusting the tightness of the membrane. At one time this was done by screws placed round the rim of the playing-surface. Today kettledrums are tuned by the operation of a pedal, which is not only more efficient but allows the player to strike his drum and then quickly adjust the tension in the membrane so as to produce a note that glides up or down in pitch. Composers have long used kettledrums not so much to keep a steady beat going as to point up certain chords and to add weight to the body of orchestral sound. Their orchestral role is therefore mainly a supporting one, although composers have occasionally given them small solo parts. Haydn's 'Drumroll' Symphony owes its nickname to the fact that it opens with a roll on the kettledrum. Beethoven opens his Violin Concerto with four notes on the kettledrums, and also makes dramatic use of them in the great scherzo of his Ninth Symphony. Gershwin brings in towards the end of his Piano Concerto in F a solo passage for

Starting young on the triangle, cymbals, tubular bells and drums (plus guitar and recorder).

kettledrums which clearly demonstrates their quality of definite pitch.

The xylophone is obviously a percussion instrument of definite pitch, its individual wooden blocks graded in size to produce a scale. The glockenspiel (German for 'bell-play'), which has metal bars; the marimba, a traditional type of Latin American xylophone; and the vibraphone, in which the sounds are sustained and modified by a special set of electrically-operated resonators (very popular in some jazz and dance music), are all based on the same principle.

The other important group of percussion instruments of definite pitch are bells. Nothing could demonstrate better the direct relationship between pitch, tone and volume of sound on the one hand, and instrumental size and shape on the other, than the contrast between the delicate tinkle of a small hand-bell and the massive, sonorous tolling of a bell weighing several tons.

Percussion instruments of indefinite pitch are more numerous. They include other types of drum—side drums (of which the medieval tabor is an early example) and the similarly constructed but larger bass drums; gongs and cymbals; the tambourine, triangle and castanets. In the orchestra it is the percussion section that also accommodates any other special-effect instruments composers sometimes ask for, even when they are not technically percussion instruments at all—from whips and rattles to car horns and wind machine (a device consisting of a broad strip of canvas stretched tightly over two large revolving cylinders or drums).

Stringed Instruments

The big division among stringed instruments is between those designed to be plucked and those whose strings are primarily intended to be set in motion by a bow.

The most ancient and widespread type of plucked stringed instrument is the harp. Fundamentally the harp consists of a set of strings stretched across a frame, each of different length (and perhaps of different thickness also), so producing notes of different pitch. The frame must also act as a resonator, giving volume and tone to the basic sound of the strings. There are many drawings or paintings of harps on the walls of Egyptian palaces or tombs, dating back thou-sands of years. A few actual specimens of these have survived. Other ancient versions of the harp are the lyre, much favoured by the Greeks, Assyrians and Hebrews, and the two main types of pre-Christian Celtic harp, the Welsh telyn and Irish clàrsach. A truly remarkable instrument was the Aeolian harp: here the strings were set in motion not by any human agent but by the action of the wind (the instrument being named after Aeolus, legendary Greek keeper of the winds). The effect is similar to that sometimes heard when the wind blows across telegraph wires, and to the Greeks, with their mystical beliefs, it was interpreted as the divine voice of the wind and of nature.

Ancient Egyptian (and one Persian) harps, illustrated in a nineteenth-century volume.

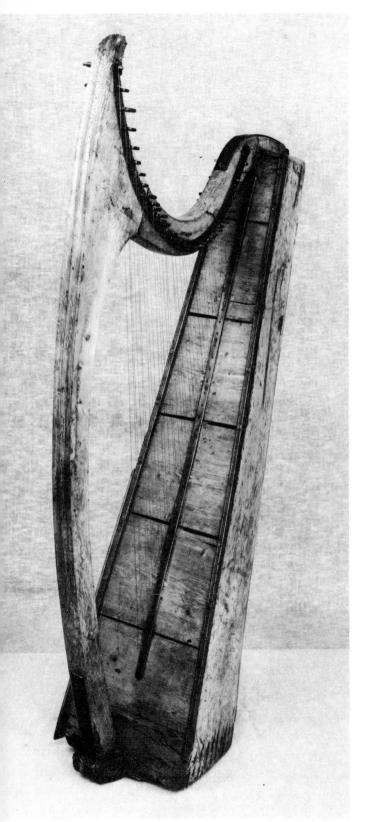

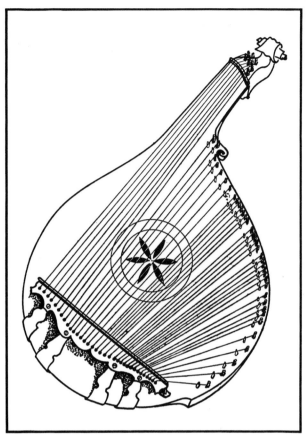

Left: A beautiful example of a traditional Irish harp.
Above: The bandoura, a traditional Russian stringed instrument.
Facing page: Pedal harp made in 1858 by the Paris firm of Erard. This famous company also made pianos.

The modern type of harp, dating from the early nineteenth century, is a large instrument with pedals which can adjust the pitch of the strings and allow the harpist a wide range of notes. It also made its way into the orchestra during the last century, adding glitter and richness to orchestral sound. Few composers have written for it as a solo instrument—Ravel's Introduction and Allegro for Flute, Harp and String Quartet being an exception—although Harpo Marx showed how attractive it could sound entirely on its own in the famous Marx Brothers films.

Above: Two eighteenth-century English citterns. These instruments are sometimes called 'English guitars'.
Left: Three characters dressed for a Renaissance play or masque. The one on the left is tuning a lute.

Other plucked stringed instruments are designed on the more familiar pattern of a neck attached to a resonating body, the strings being stretched down the length of the instrument. Such instruments do not have a separate string for each note. Instead, the player adjusts the effective playing length of a limited number of strings by pressing them against the neck at selected points with the fingers of one hand, a process called stopping. By Renaissance times there were plucked stringed instruments of a wide range called citterns and theorbos. Above all there was the lute, which inspired some of the finest instrumental music of the period. Today, the best-known plucked stringed instrument is the guitar, whose direct ancestor was the Spanish vihuela. Others are the mandolin (similar to a

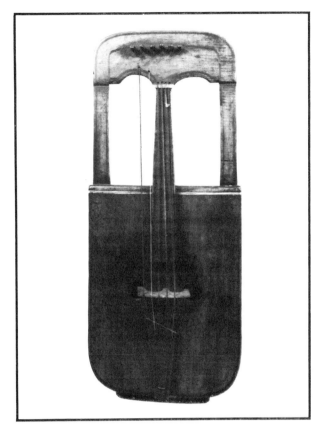

Above: The Celtic crwth, one of the earliest types of stringed instruments played with a bow.
Right: Handsome cello (violoncello), dated 1711, made by the School of Stradivarius.

lute), the banjo, the ukelele and the Russian balalaika.

A very early example of a bowed stringed instrument was the old Celtic crwth, dating back to at least the sixth century AD; but the ancestor of most other bowed instruments was the medieval rebec, which probably made its way into Europe from the Middle East. Rebecs were made in a variety of sizes, the size of the instrument being directly related to its range of notes.

The first important family of bowed instruments were the viols, including closely related instruments like the viola d'amore. Viols had six strings, attached to tuning-pegs at the end of the neck and raised above the body of the instrument by a curved section of wood called a bridge. They also had frets (little raised strips of wood or metal, as in a guitar) inserted down the neck to aid stopping. They were normally placed on the player's knee (except for the larger versions, which were supported between the knees), the bow being drawn gently across their strings with the palm of the hand facing outwards. To modern ears, hearing them for the first time, viols may seem to produce a rather constrained, pinched sort of sound. But it is a sound that grows more attractive with acquaintance, and one that was perfectly suited to the polyphonic music popular in Renaissance times. It was not until about 1700 that the viol was finally superseded by the violin.

A violin, compared in shape and construction to a viol, has a longer, narrower neck, higher shoulders to the body and a rounded back. Most important of all, its strings (four in number) are tighter strung and supported by a stronger, more rounded bridge. From the start, these features, taken in conjunction with new methods of using the bow, gave the violin a brighter tone and stronger musical 'attack'; and further developments, notably in the lengthening of the neck and strengthening of the bow, improved these qualities. Playing styles for the instrument have also changed. In earlier days it was often pressed against the performer's chest rather than tucked under the chin, which did not give him such quick control over the instrument. The viola, cello and double-bass are, in all important respects, larger versions of the violin, giving to

Below: French gentleman of Louis XIV's time playing a bass viol, sometimes called in Italian *viola da gamba* because it was placed between the legs like a cello.
Right: Fine grouping of the violin family, from a nineteenth-century musical manual.

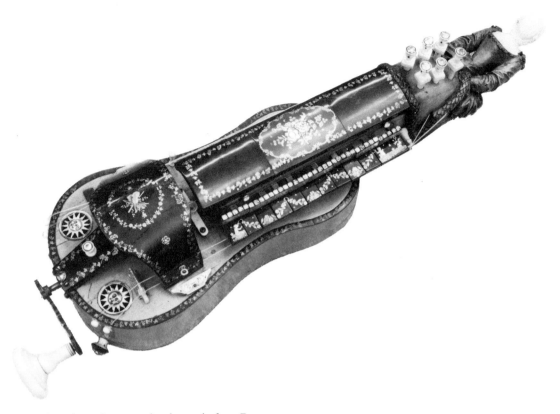

Beautifully made eighteenth-century hurdy-gurdy from France.

each a successively lower-pitched range of notes; but there is also a difference of thickness, and sometimes of material, in the strings, from one instrument to the next, and this too has its effect on pitch and tone.

The home of the violin was Italy, and the earliest models date from about the middle of the sixteenth century. The first great period of production was centred on the town of Cremona and the craftsmanship of several families of instrument-makers—the Stradivaris, Guarneris and Amatis. The first generation of important composers for the violin were also Italians— Corelli, Torelli, Vivaldi. Since the time of Bach and Handel, the violin family have provided the foundation of orchestral sound, being also numerically the largest section of almost any orchestra. As solo instruments, the violin and cello have been most popular with composers, though the viola has had its champions, including Berlioz, Hindemith (who was a viola player) and Walton. In chamber music, the beautifully balanced combination of the string quartet— two violins, viola and cello—has inspired some of the greatest music from composers as different as Haydn, Mozart, Beethoven, Bartók and Shostakovich.

Two interesting variants of the bowed stringed instrument group are the tromba marina, which was a very tall one-stringed instrument, and the hurdy-gurdy. In the hurdy-gurdy a set of strings is laid across one segment of a wheel. The player turns the handle of the wheel, which activates the strings, while stopping them with his other hand to produce different notes. The continuous motion of the wheel against the strings produces a droning effect. There are medieval prints which show very large hurdy-gurdies being laid across the laps of two men, one turning the wheel, the other stopping the strings. Other varieties of the instrument have been elaborately constructed with a set of keys for the player to depress in order to stop the strings more easily than by manual control.

Woodwind Instruments

Woodwind instruments were at one time all actually made of wood. Today, some instruments classed as 'woodwind' are, in fact, made of metal, and the real distinction between woodwind and brass instruments lies not in their materials but in their design and methods of playing.

The basis of a woodwind instrument is either a tube which the player blows across or into at an angle in order to start the column of air inside vibrating, or a tube which amplifies and modifies the vibrations of a thin reed attached to one end. The other distinctive feature shared by virtually all woodwind instruments is that they have holes along the side of the tube, which the player covers or uncovers to alter the effective playing length of the instrument and so obtain notes of different pitch. It is possible to produce more than one note on any wind instrument just by blowing harder and so obtaining different notes in the basic harmonic series; but without the holes in a woodwind instrument the range of notes would be very limited and uncertain.

The recorder, very popular in Renaissance times, is a relatively simple woodwind instrument of the first type described above. The flute (like its smaller, higher-pitched companion the piccolo) is another which requires the player to blow across a mouthpiece, to activate the column of air inside the tube. As with early types of harp, so there are many ancient Egyptian pictures of flute-players. Some are shown holding the instrument downwards and blowing across one end. Others are playing the much more common transverse flute, holding the instrument sideways and blowing into a mouthpiece in its side. The modern type of flute owes its existence to the nineteenth-century German flute-player

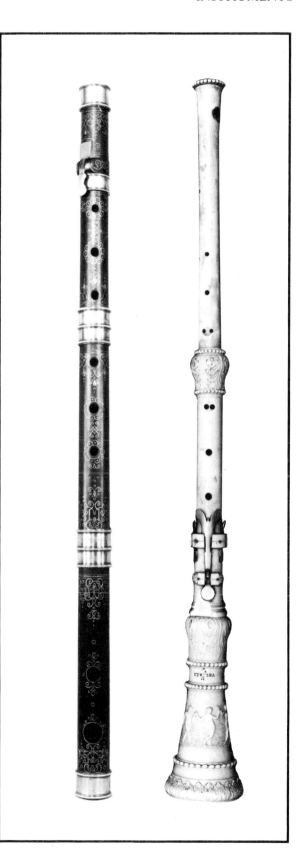

Facing page: Four treble recorders of the eighteenth and nineteenth centuries. The one on the left is Italian, veneered with tortoiseshell and inlaid with gold pique and mother of pearl.
Right: Early eighteenth-century English flute, made of ebony and mounted in silver.
Far right: Italian oboe of the early eighteenth century.

Theobald Boehm. Before his time the positioning of the holes in the side was limited by the ability of the player to cover them with his fingers. Boehm re-designed the instrument, placing holes in the best position from the point of view of its own acoustics, at the same time making them possible to cover and uncover without great difficulty by a system of keys and levers. The pure, sometimes melancholy, sometimes rather sensual sound of the flute (especially in its lower registers) has always attracted musicians. The instrument was very popular in the eighteenth century, Frederick the Great of Prussia being an enthusiast. In orchestral music there is a prominent part for the flute in the scherzo of Mendelssohn's incidental music to *A Midsummer Night's Dream*, and the famous flute solo that opens Debussy's *Prélude à l'Après-midi d'un faune*.

The oboe's ancestors were the shawms, pommers and curtalls of the Middle Ages and Renaissance period. Its immediate predecessor was an instrument called, in French, *hautbois* ('loud wood'). The instrument as we know it today emerged during the latter part of the eighteenth century, in the time of Haydn and Mozart. It is classed as a double-reed instrument, having two thin narrow reeds which form the actual mouthpiece and vibrate against each other. Modern versions are equipped with keys and levers for the operation of the holes, based on the Boehm system. In orchestral music, the slightly larger, deeper-toned *cor anglais* ('English horn', though, confusingly, it has nothing specially to do with England and is not a horn) has tended to steal the limelight in solo passage work, the best-known example being the long opening theme to Berlioz's *Carnaval Romain* overture. Richard Strauss, however, composed a fine oboe concerto.

Closely related to the oboe (using a double reed) but with a distinctive sound of its own is the bassoon. One of its ancestors was the racket, in which the long tube of the instrument was coiled up inside a cylindrical box for convenient handling. A consort of rackets (a set of differently sized instruments) sounds rather like a group of melodious bees. The Italian word for bassoon, *fagotto*, meaning 'bundle', is a rather uncomplimentary way of describing how the long tube of the instrument is bent round itself. Its rather pawky tone in the middle registers has tended to cast the bassoon in a comic role in the orchestra, as in Dukas's light-hearted symphonic poem *L'Apprenti sorcier*. It can, however, be made to sound very forlorn, as it does at the beginning of

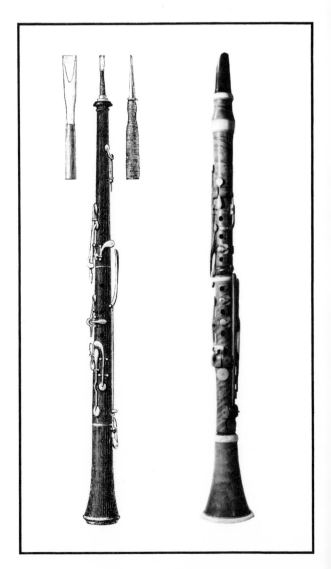

Right: French oboe (*hautbois*) of the late nineteenth century.
Far right: Clarinet of pear wood, with ivory rings and brass keys, made in England about 1840.

Tchaikovsky's 'Pathétique' Symphony, or bleak and desolate, as at the beginning of Stravinsky's *The Rite of Spring*. The bassoon can reach quite low notes. The more recently invented double-bassoon, or contra-bassoon, can play a whole octave lower and so plunge down to the very depths of orchestral sound. Ravel uses it to portray the beast in the Beauty and the Beast movement of his *Mother Goose* suite.

Though there were earlier woodwind instruments similar to it, the clarinet started life very much in its own right at around the beginning of the eighteenth century. It has a single reed which vibrates against the mouthpiece. The modern instrument is equipped with levers and keys for the holes, again based on the Boehm system. It exists in various forms, tuned to particular keys, but the only variant with a real difference is the bass clarinet, which looks a little like a saxophone, and produces a dark, sinewy tone. Mozart, inspired by the playing of Anton Stadler, was the first composer to write great music for the clarinet—his Clarinet Quintet (K581) and Clarinet Concerto (K622). He also had a great affection for the deeper-toned basset horn (again, it has no connection with a true horn). Brahms and Weber have been two other outstanding composers for the clarinet. It has also figured prominently in jazz, in the hands of such famous instrumentalists as Sidney Bechet, Woody Herman, Benny Goodman and Artie Shaw. Generally the instrument has an open, easy sound, but in its upper registers it can sound quite frightening. Richard Strauss uses it in this way in his symphonic poem *Till Eulenspiegel* to depict the hero being strung up on a gallows.

The saxophone is generally classed as a woodwind instrument, because it has a reed and a woodwind-type arrangement of holes operated by levers and keys, although the tube itself is fashioned more like that of a brass instrument. It was invented by the Belgian Adolphe Sax in the last century, originally to add power to the woodwind section of French military bands. A few composers, notably Bizet and Vaughan Williams, have included passages for it in their orchestral music; and a small group of saxophones (made to different sizes—soprano, tenor, alto) can sound charming. But the instrument really came into its own in the field of jazz and dance music. Some of the greatest jazz players have been saxophonists—Charlie Parker, Lester Young, Coleman Hawkins, Gerry Mulligan, Stan Getz.

The bagpipes have long been associated with Scotland, but are one of the most ancient and widely distributed of woodwind-type instruments. The most distinctive feature of bagpipes is the bag or sack (traditionally made from the bladder or stomach of a sheep or goat) which acts as a reservoir for air. The player blows into this

Albrecht Dürer's famous engraving of a bagpiper, dated 1514.

(or in some cases supplies it with a pair of bellows) then directs the air into a set of small pipes equipped with some kind of reed. The bagpipes probably originated somewhere in Asia, thousands of years ago. They are still found, in various forms, in many parts of the Middle East and Europe. The celebrated Scottish Highland bagpipes are a powerful instrument with a strong, strident tone, best heard in the open air. Other types, such as the Northumbrian pipes, have a much gentler, more mellifluous tone.

Brass Instruments

Brass instruments (usually but not always made of that metal) operate in quite a different way from woodwind instruments. The player presses his lips to one end of the metal tube and spits into the instrument. It is possible to obtain a note from a metal tube by blowing straight into it in the manner described, but all brass instruments are fitted with a cup- or funnel-shaped mouthpiece which allows the player much greater control over the pitch and tone. At the other end they are characterized by the way the tube opens out into what is called the bell.

Trumpets, the brass instruments most people first think of, have changed very little in their basic musical character for thousands of years. A type of trumpet found in the tomb of the Egyptian pharaoh Tutankhamun has the same fundamentally high, clear, penetrating sound as any trumpet heard today. This quality traditionally gave the trumpet an important role in signalling and in military operations, where it could be clearly heard above the sound of battle. Its bright, silvery tone also made it ideal for ceremonial fanfares. In the eighteenth century composers like Bach and Handel sometimes wrote very high-pitched trumpet parts, called clarino parts, requiring specialized skill on the instruments of their day. Until the nineteenth century the trumpet consisted of one long tube, extending in a straight line, or bent round itself for easier handling. In this form the player could extract from it only the basic notes of its natural harmonics. The famous trumpet call in Beethoven's *Leonora no 3* overture demonstrates this

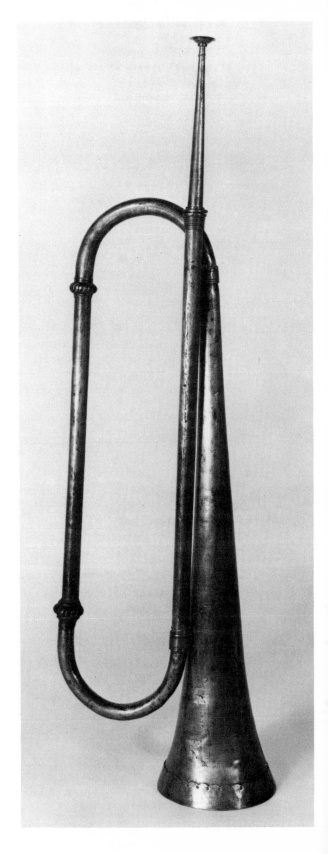

The Scout and Guide Band.

A drummer at the Jamaica Carifesta.

classic type of trumpet playing. During the last century, however, it was equipped with piston-operated valves to cut off or add sections to its playing length, thus greatly extending its range of notes. The bugle, smaller in size and without valves, and the cornet, with valves, are closely related to the standard trumpet. This century the trumpet has flourished in jazz, in the hands of such widely different musicians as Louis Armstrong, Dizzy Gillespie and Miles Davis; while the cornet, with its rounder tone, was 'Bix' Beiderbecke's favoured instrument.

The trombone is easily recognizable by its sliding valve mechanism, which shortens or increases the playing length of the instrument at will. In Renaissance and Baroque times it was known in England as the sackbut. The instrument has a full, rounded tone. It was much used in church music up to the eighteenth century. Mozart was one of the first to use trombones in the orchestra, in his opera *Don Giovanni*. Beethoven was the first to use them in a symphony (his Fifth). As with the trumpet, so the trombone has figured prominently this century in jazz, through the talents of Edward 'Kid' Ory, Jack Teagarden and swing band leaders Tommy Dorsey and Glenn Miller.

The horn, called in full the French horn, is basically rounded in shape, with a very wide bell. An ancient ancestor was the Scandinavian lur,

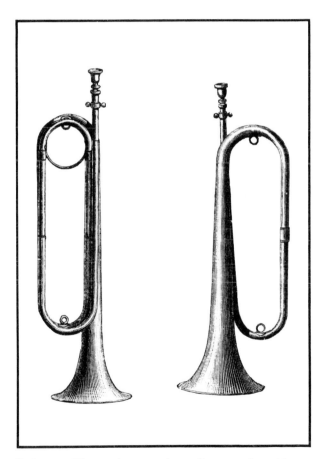

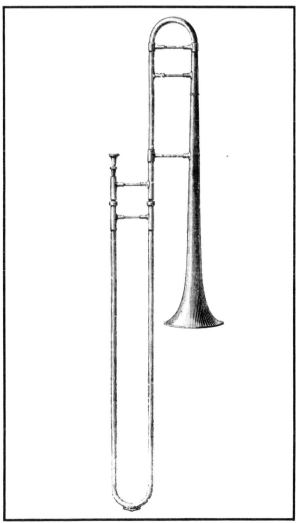

Facing page: Nineteenth-century 'natural' trumpet (i.e. without valves or crooks) from India. Note the relatively narrow 'bell'.
Above: Trumpet (left) and bugle, illustrated in a nineteenth-century manual.
Right: Nineteenth-century trombone with its familiar sliding valve.

Eighteenth-century engraving showing the manufacture of hunting horns. The craftsman at the back is filling a tube with molten lead to soften the metal and allow it to be fashioned into its circular shape.

made of bronze, but the horn as we think of it started off as a hunting instrument, and its romantic association with woods and fields is enhanced by its rather haunting, mellow tones. The old hunting horn consisted simply of a coiled tube, and like early trumpets was only capable of sounding the notes of its harmonic series. In the eighteenth century horns were provided with detachable sections called crooks. By adding or removing a crook the player altered the playing length of his instrument, so changing its harmonic range from one key to another. By the middle of the nineteenth century, crooks were superseded by piston valves, giving the horn, like the valve trumpet, much greater melodic freedom. The horn is the oldest brass instrument to have a regular place in the orchestra, and has been given more prominence than others. Mozart and Richard Strauss (whose father was a horn player) have written fine concertos for it. Famous horn solos in larger orchestral works

occur in the slow movement of Tchaikovsky's Fifth Symphony, and at the opening of Richard Strauss's *Till Eulenspiegel*. Berlioz also makes very imaginative use of the horn to suggest the tolling of a bell in the slow movement of his 'Harold in Italy' Symphony. Horns have also been used with great effect in ensemble work, as by Beethoven in the trio section to the scherzo of his 'Eroica' Symphony and by Wagner to depict King Mark's departure for the hunt in *Tristan und Isolde*.

In the modern orchestra the tuba is the deepest-toned brass instrument in regular use—a large, hefty instrument with an exceedingly wide bell and large, conical-bored tube equipped with piston valves, which the player rests on his lap, bell facing upwards. Like the double bass, the tuba almost always plays a supporting role in orchestral music, though Vaughan Williams wrote a concerto for it. Very similar is the euphonium, used in many military and brass bands.

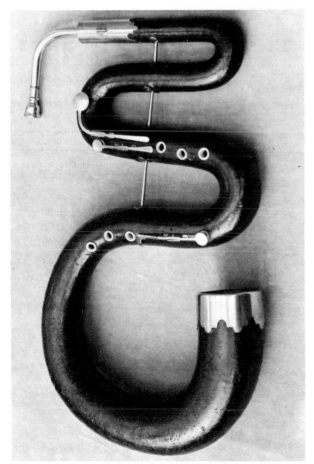

Tubas constructed in a circular fashion are called helicons, a particular example being the sousaphone, named after the American military band leader and composer Sousa. The sousaphone was also included in many early jazz bands, later being replaced by a string bass. The so-called Wagner tuba, designed by the composer for use in some of his music dramas, is, in fact, closer to a horn in construction and sound.

A now obsolete but interesting variant of a brass instrument is the appropriately named serpent. This was related to an even earlier type of wind instrument called the cornett which had a wooden, or sometimes ivory, tube with holes (like a woodwind instrument) but a small, cup-shaped mouthpiece like brass instruments. The serpent itself was made of either wood or metal (and usually covered with leather). It was popular both in church and in military bands, up until about the middle of the last century.

Wind bands generally have a long and interesting history. In the eighteenth and nineteenth centuries they usually consisted of oboes, clarinets, bassoons and horns, and inspired a few really great pieces of music (called *Harmoniemusik* in German), notably Mozart's wind serenades in B flat (K361) and in C minor (K388). Gounod also wrote a very attractive 'Petite Symphonie' for wind band.

Top: Nineteenth-century horn with a beautifully decorated 'bell'.
Above: A well-preserved example of the serpent.

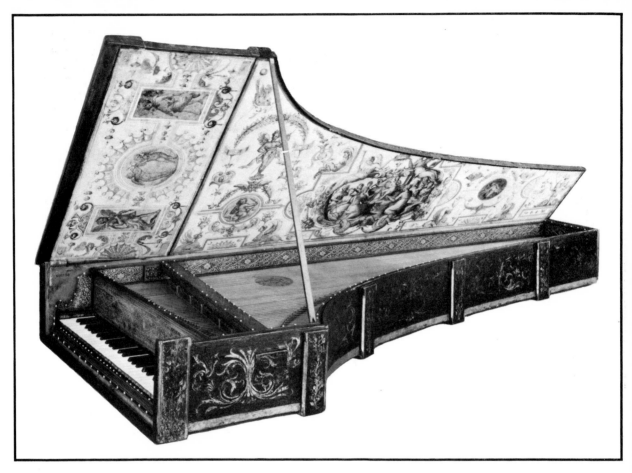

Magnificently decorated Italian harpsichord dated 1574.

Keyboard Instruments

A keyboard—the arrangement of levers or keys that activate the source of sound—is what links together a variety of instruments that might otherwise be variously classed as stringed instruments, wind or percussion.

The largest group of stringed keyboard instruments were the various forms of harpsichord. Their construction was based on that of much simpler instruments like the psaltery and dulcimer, which had a set of strings stretched over a sounding-board (i.e. resonator). Depression of the keys operated a device called a jack which plucked the strings. The virginal was the simplest type of harpsichord. At one time the name was fancifully believed to be connected with Elizabeth I (the 'Virgin Queen'), since the instru-

ment was very popular during her reign. The much more likely origin is the Latin word *virga* meaning a rod or jack, which forms an important part of its mechanism. Similar to it was the spinet. Both these instruments had their strings positioned horizontally along the length of the keyboard, or at a slight angle to it. The big difference with the true harpsichord was the placing of the strings in a direct line away from the keyboard. This difference in design gave the harpsichord more strength and volume of sound than the virginal and spinet. The most famous manufacturers of harpsichords were the Ruckers family of Antwerp during the seventeenth century. Bach and Handel, Couperin and Rameau all wrote great keyboard music for the instrument. Earlier this century such music was often

A modern Steinway concert grand piano.

played on a piano, but, with a revival of interest in the harpsichord, it is today again played on the instrument for which it was written.

The other stringed keyboard instrument, dating back like the harpsichords to Renaissance times, was the clavichord. This was equipped with a mechanism which struck the strings instead of plucking them, and for this reason can be considered the forerunner of the piano. What made the mechanism of the piano a real technical advance was the fact that the hammer struck the string and immediately bounced off again, leaving the string free to vibrate. Its inventor was the Italian Bartolommeo Cristofori, in about the year 1710. He called his early models incorporating this mechanism *gravicembalo col piano e forte* ('harpsichord with softness and loudness') to em-

phasize their new and greater dynamic range. The name became shortened in time to *piano-forte*, and then to *piano*—'soft'. In fact, it took the remainder of the eighteenth century for the piano to supersede the harpsichord, and nearly another hundred years—that is, up to about 1900—for it to emerge as the instrument we know today. Important landmarks in its development were the introduction of more strings and a wider keyboard; and the introduction of the upright piano (i.e. one with vertically placed strings) in about 1800 by the American manufacturer John Hawkins of Philadelphia. Of even greater significance was Hawkins's use of an iron frame which allowed the strings to be held in a far higher degree of tension and so to be capable of producing a fuller, stronger tone when hit.

Other famous piano manufacturers have been John Broadwood of London, Pleyel of Paris, Bösendorfer of Vienna, Bechstein of Berlin, and Steinway of New York. From about the middle of the eighteenth century many of the greatest composers have written for the piano of their time—C.P.E. and J.C. Bach, Haydn, Mozart, Beethoven, Schumann, Chopin, Brahms, Liszt, Debussy and Ravel—thus providing it with the richest, most varied musical literature of any single instrument.

The organ is basically a set of pipes—usually of two types, the so-called flue pipes constructed something like a whistle, and the more complex reed pipes—attached to a reservoir of air called a wind chest. Depression of the keys operates a mechanism that allows air from the wind chest to blow into the corresponding pipes and so produce notes. The history of the instrument dates back to the second or third century BC, and to the invention of an intriguing kind of organ called a hydraulus. This, as its Greek name suggests, involved the use of water to pump air into the wind chest and maintain it at a fairly constant pressure. The Egyptians, Greeks and Romans all had versions of the hydraulus, and several representations of it have survived, though exactly how it worked is now something of a mystery.

The earliest organs of the Christian era, dating from about the ninth century, were not really keyboard instruments, because slots of wood called sliders had to be pulled or pushed to control the passage of air into the pipes. A very large organ of about this time, installed in Winchester Cathedral, apparently needed over fifty men to operate it—to work both the sliders and the giant bellows supplying it with air. For some time to come organs remained rather clumsy affairs, early keyboards consisting of broad wooden keys which needed to be thumped hard with the fist to make them work. During the later Middle Ages and Renaissance periods there were two varieties of the instrument: the portative organ, which was small enough to be carried about, and the larger positive organ.

Organs dating from the seventeenth century set the pattern for future development, with one or more keyboards (or manuals), an additional pedal board of long wooden levers (a German invention), and stops contained in panels by the side of the keyboards which allowed the player to select whole sets of pipes with particular sound qualities. The German Silbermann family, well known to Bach, made some of the finest organs of the Baroque period (as well as harpsichords and clavichords). In the nineteenth century, as a symbol of the wealth and advancing technology of the Industrial Revolution, some mammoth instruments were made. Earlier this century there was also the cinema organ, operated electronically, which included many novel sound effects. In terms of serious organ building, there has been a return this century to the fairly modest size of the Baroque instruments. Bach's organ

Engraving of a fifteenth-century positive organ. Note the bellows.

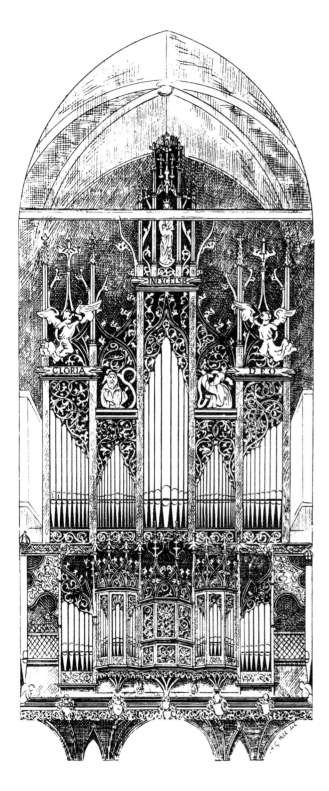

The splendid sixteenth-century organ in the Marienkirche, Lübeck, where Buxtehude was organist (see page 130).

music was the greatest written for the instrument. For over a hundred years after his death the organ was neglected by most composers, but this century more important music has been added to its repertory, especially by composers like Messiaen, who have added to the long tradition of French organ music.

There are a variety of instruments belonging to what is called the reed-organ family. Usually they have no pipes, the sound coming directly from freely vibrating reeds. An early example, dating from Renaissance times, was a very small kind of portable organ called a regal. One version of this, the Bible regal, could be opened and closed like a book. More recent members of this family include the mouth organ or harmonica, the accordion and concertina. There is also the harmonium with a keyboard and bellows pumped by the player's feet. None of these instruments has risen to great musical heights, but Dvořák was one composer who had a soft spot for the harmonium, while the American Larry Adler has shown how much fine music can be played on the harmonica.

Mechanical Instruments

These operate without direct human control. In the past they have usually been driven by some sort of clockwork, while an apparatus known as 'barrel-and-pin' has been most widely used as the actual agent of their performance. This is an accurate enough description of a barrel or cylinder carefully fitted with pegs or pins. As the barrel revolves the pins activate the levers, pulleys, stops or other devices which control the source of sound. As long ago as the fourteenth century, the barrel-and-pin principle was applied to the chiming of bells. By the sixteenth century barrel-and-pin mechanisms were being installed in virginals and organs. Elizabeth I is reported to have sent the Sultan of Turkey a mechanical instrument of this kind which could play a continuous selection of pieces for nearly seven hours. The barrel-and-pin mechanism has been applied to musical clocks and to musical boxes. Here the revolving pattern of pins strikes a row of little metal bars, their graded length producing a range of notes. An interesting variant of this was the nineteenth-century polyphon, designed to play metal discs with a pattern of pins or notches inscribed on them. As the disc revolved, so the notches activated the striking of the tuned metal bars. The discs were detachable, so giving the owner a choice of music, and anticipating the idea of the modern record disc.

A newer method of mechanical production has been the perforated roll, usually made of specially stiffened paper. Instead of pins or pegs, the perforations in the roll operate the instrument pneumatically (that is, with the aid of air, or perhaps of steam). Most mechanical fairground steam organs, or calliopes, have worked on this principle. So have mechanical pianos, called pianolas or player pianos. In their case the perforated-roll technique proved efficient enough for some great pianists to 'cut' rolls

which would accurately reproduce their performance. Pianolas or other types of reproducing pianos usually have keyboards like any normal instrument, so that as the rolls are fed into them the individual keys, operated from within, move rather uncannily up and down as though at the command of some ghostly, unseen hand.

Some mechanical instruments have been very elaborate. Johann Maelzel, who produced an early type of metronome (a mechanical device using a sort of inverted pendulum to indicate tempo speeds), also invented the Panharmonicon, which was like a whole mechanical orchestra. Beethoven was friendly with Maelzel and composed his piece called *The Battle of Victoria* (also known, in the version for a normal orchestra, as the 'Battle Symphony') for the Panharmonicon.

Small mechanically operated organ showing very clearly its barrel-and-pin mechanism. Note the percussive effects of bell and triangle.

The Voice

This is the instrument as old as humanity itself, but continually new. None of us needs to be told how to use it—we usually demonstrate this within moments of being born—but we can all get much more out of it with care and training. The voice cannot be directly compared with any man-made instrument. The source of its sound is in the larynx, in the front of the throat. Attached to the larynx are the vocal chords. These are membranes—a little over a centimetre long in an adult male, slightly less in women and children—which we automatically tighten when we wish to use our voice, so that the air we breathe out from the lungs and up the windpipe makes them vibrate and produce sound. Other parts of our anatomy—chest and neck, mouth and nose (including the sinus cavities above the nose)—then act as a complex resonator, amplifying and shaping the pitch and tone of our vocal chords. How differently these factors affect the voice can be understood by comparing the traditional Eastern way of singing, which is largely through the nose, with the Western tradition of opening the mouth wide.

The origins of song—using the word in this

The Westminster Abbey choir representing the age-old combination of boys' and men's voices.

context to include all kinds of chants, laments and war cries—is lost in history. People almost certainly used their voice in what might be considered some form of musical expression before they developed proper speech, and before they had invented any other instruments that we might recognize as such. As far as the beginnings of European or Western music are concerned, the voice played a far more important part than any other instrument for several hundred years—in the singing of church plainsong and other forms of chanting. And when church vocal music began to lose its lead during the late Middle Ages and the Renaissance, so opera, oratorio and song emerged to keep the voice in the forefront of music.

Musically, voices are classified according to their range of notes. In the case of women they are soprano (the highest-pitched), mezzo-soprano (half-soprano, or not quite so high) and contralto. In men the basic division is between tenor (the highest-pitched), baritone and bass. Boys' voices are considered differently, being defined as treble or alto. When they 'break' it means that the vocal chords are growing larger and tougher, together with the throat muscles and other related parts of the body. It is the musical sign of approaching manhood. In the past, when the church did not permit the use of women's voices, boys were sometimes castrated to deny them full manhood and so keep their voices unbroken. The object was to combine the soprano tone with the power and control of a man's pair of lungs. Such singers—often very famous and successful—were known as castrati. It is, however, possible for a normal man to speak or sing in a falsetto voice (like a boy), and with care and training some male singers, called counter-tenors, can come very close to the sound of a true castrato.

These long-established divisions between different types of voice, male and female, are not so important in jazz, dance and pop music. This is partly because of the character of the music itself, and partly because since the 1920s nearly all such vocalists have used microphones as an essential part of their performance. Clever and creative use of the microphone allows them to project a vocal personality that is usually more important than the intrinsic nature or quality of their voice.

Cleo Laine, one of today's most versatile and attractive jazz vocalists.

Electrophonic Instruments

The microphone, as used by vocalists, is an example of the way the production of musical sound has been revolutionized during this century by electrical means. In the case of the microphone, an electrical device is being used in conjunction with an existing instrument—the voice. The partnership between a conventional instrument and electrical appliances has been developed in various other ways. In the Neo-Bechstein piano, for example, the strings of the instrument are set vibrating by the conventional use of hammers, but their vibrations are then picked up, amplified and modified electrically, the sound finally being delivered through loudspeakers. The Vierling violin is played in the usual way, but is similarly wired for sound. In the last thirty years the guitar has become the most popular of such electrically-aided instruments, bearing little resemblance to a 'classical' guitar, because its shape and size have relatively little to do with its sound reproduction.

True electrophonic instruments are those in which the source of sound is also electronic. An early and well-known example is the American-designed Hammond Organ, which has a conventional keyboard, but no pipes. The sounds are created, modified and amplified entirely by electronic means. In the case of the Hammond Organ and similar designs, the resulting sounds still resemble those of an existing instrument. Other electrophonic instruments, whose sound source is usually some type of electrical valve oscillator or oscillators, can produce sounds which are radically different from those heard on any conventional instrument. Well before the Second World War there was already a wide range of such devices. One of these was the *Ondes Martenot*, or Martenot Waves, named after its French inventor Maurice Martenot. This is activated by a normal keyboard, but produces a succession of notes which are remarkably pure, rather unearthly in tone, and belonging to a realm of sound beyond that of normal musical acoustics.

Since the war electrophonic music has become important to many composers. The magnetic

One of the most up-to-date electronic synthesizers in use today. This one is called an EMS Synthi 100.

recording tape has enabled them to take quite ordinary sounds and transform them, by a process of play-backs, re-recordings and cutting, into the most extraordinary sound patterns. Even more significant has been the arrival on the scene of the synthesizer. The word 'synthesize' means to bring together, to build up, and the apparatus can start with basic sound oscillations and build them up, by the most complex electronic analysis of wave patterns and overtones, to imitate conventional instruments, or to create sounds right outside the province of normal experience. Electrophonic engineers and composers who use synthesizers need to know about the scientific 'anatomy' of sound—of the action and interaction of overtones and harmonics, of the physical properties of different types of sound wave, and of the so-called 'decay' of sound. Just as a synthesizer can build up sounds, so it can take them apart, filtering them and stripping them layer by layer of their overtones and harmonics, until there is nothing left but the hiss known as 'white' sound. Thus can one person create a universe of sound, as astonishing as any trip into space, and dissolve it again, just with the touch of his fingers.

Musicians

Adam de la Halle
(about 1231–88).
Most famous of the poet-musicians called *trouvères* who lived in France during the Middle Ages. He wrote a play with music called the *Jeu de Robin et Marion*, which anticipated certain kinds of opera by nearly five hundred years.

Albéniz, Isaac (1860–1909).
Spanish composer and pianist. As a child prodigy he studied with Liszt, then travelled widely and lived mainly in London and Paris. As a composer Albéniz made great use of the traditional rhythms and harmonies of his own country and was an important figure in the Spanish nationalist school of music. His compositions include a set of piano pieces, each representing a different region of Spain, called collectively *Iberia*; and a very popular Tango.

Armstrong, Louis 'Satchmo'
(1900–71).
American jazz trumpeter, whose early career sounds very like the early history of jazz itself. He joined Edward 'Kid' Ory's New Orleans band in 1918, then played for a period on Mississippi riverboats before joining Joe 'King' Oliver's band in Chicago. Armstrong later became a great show-business personality, appearing in many films, so winning a big new audience for his kind of 'traditional' jazz.

Arne, Thomas Augustine
(1710–78).
English composer, mainly of operas and other stage works with music. These are rarely performed today, but he remains famous as composer of the song 'Rule, Britannia' (first heard as a part of one of his masques). His son Michael wrote another song which is still popular, 'The Lass with the Delicate Air'.

Bach, Johann Sebastian
(1685–1750).
German composer and organist. Born in Eisenach, Thuringia (now in East Germany), he held various posts as organist, choirmaster and director of music, the last of these being at the school and church of St Thomas (*Thomasschule*) in Leipzig, where he died. Bach won great fame as an organist, but as a composer he was not highly rated by most of his contemporaries and his music was neglected for many years afterwards. Now he is recognized, with Handel, as the last great composer of the Baroque period and the last great master of polyphonic styles of music. He composed in virtually every form of his time, except opera, his work falling into three main categories: (1) compositions for the organ— fantasias, chorales, preludes and fugues; (2) orchestral and instrumental music—the 'Brandenburg' Concertos and other concerto-style works (some being arrangements of music by other composers), the

Forty-eight Preludes and Fugues for the keyboard (also called *Das wolhtemperierte Clavier*), the 'Goldberg' Variations, numerous suites and partitas, *The Musical Offering* (for Frederick the Great of Prussia) and *The Art of Fugue* (which exists in several versions); (3) choral works— nearly 300 church cantatas (from one of which comes the well-known piece known as 'Jesu, Joy of Man's Desiring'), some secular cantatas (including the 'Coffee' Cantata), the Christmas Oratorio, St John and St Matthew Passions, and Mass in B minor. This immense output has been catalogued and indexed by the German scholar Wolfgang Schmieder, and individual works are now often quoted with their BWV number—*Bach Werke-Verzeichnis* ('Index of Bach's Works'). Of Bach's twenty children by his two marriages, three of his sons became important musical figures in their own right. Wilhelm Friedemann (1710–84), the eldest son, was a highly gifted man and composer of much fine organ and keyboard music, but was not successful and died in poverty. Carl Philipp Emanuel (1714–88), for some years court musician to Frederick the Great, wrote symphonies and sonatas in the new Classical style of his time, his keyboard pieces being especially interesting for the way they mark the change in style from composition for the harpsichord to that for the much newer piano. Johann Christian

(1735–82) settled in London, henceforth being known as the 'English Bach' or 'London Bach'. He wrote operas, also symphonies and piano concertos in the new Classical style, and gave some lessons to Mozart when he visited London as a child.

Balakirev, Mily (1837–1910). Russian composer and founder-member of the group of Russian nationalist composers known as 'The Five'. He wrote two symphonies, a symphonic poem, and much piano music including the fantasy *Islamey* which is strongly Asiatic in mood. There is an orchestral version of this.

Barber, Samuel (born 1910). American composer whose music is generally quite traditional and lyrical in style. His works include two sym-phonies, the opera *Vanessa* (with a libretto by his American colleague Gian-Carlo Menotti), the ballet *Medea* and the very well-known Adagio for Strings (originally the slow movement of a string quartet).

Bartók, Béla (1881–1945). Hungarian composer whose intensive study of Hungarian and Romanian folk music largely shaped his own very original style and made him a major figure of twentieth-century music. His works include the opera *Duke Bluebeard's Castle*, the ballet *The Miraculous Mandarin*, three piano concertos, two violin concertos, Music for Strings, Percussion and Celesta, Concerto for Orchestra, six string quartets, and much music for the piano, notably *Mikrokosmos* (over 150 pieces of graded technical difficulty) and the suite *Out of Doors*. Soon after the outbreak of the Second World War Bartók emigrated to the United States, but despite his fame his last years were sad and lonely ones.

Basie, William 'Count' (born 1904). American jazz musician and, from the 1930s to the 1960s, one of the leading figures of 'big band' or 'mainstream' jazz. His bands, usually directed by him from the piano, were famed for their musical precision and 'attack' and strong rhythmic drive. His early composition 'One O'Clock Jump' also became his signature tune.

Below: Count Basie in concert

Béla Bartók

Beethoven, Ludwig van

(1770–1827).

German composer. He was born in Bonn but as a young man settled permanently in Vienna (where he died). His career as a pianist was ruined by approaching deafness, and from then on he concentrated on composition, dramatically enlarging the Classical forms of the symphony, concerto, string quartet and sonata and greatly increasing the expressive power of music. By his fiercely independent spirit, and despite deafness and frequent ill-health, he also raised the stature of the artist in society. Through his work, attitudes and way of life Beethoven can thus be seen as the great dividing figure between the Classical eighteenth century and the Romantic nineteenth century, and his influence on music has been enormous. His principal works are: nine symphonies—no 1 in C major (opus 21), no 2 in D major (opus 36), no 3 in E flat ('Eroica', opus 55), no 4 in B flat (opus 60), no 5 in C minor (opus 67), no 6 in F major ('Pastoral', opus 68), no 7 in A major (opus 92), no 8 in F major (opus 93), no 9 in D minor ('Choral', opus 125); five piano concertos—no 5 in E flat (opus 73) being nicknamed 'Emperor'; Violin Concerto in D (opus 61); the opera *Fidelio* (originally called *Leonora*); Mass in D (*Missa Solemnis*, opus 123); overture and incidental music to Goethe's play *Egmont*; sixteen string quartets, including the six of opus 18, the three of opus 59 (known as the 'Rassumovsky' Quartets), and the group composed at the end of his life, plus the separately published *Grosse Fuge* (opus 133); thirty-two piano sonatas, including no 8 in C minor ('Pathétique', opus 13), no 14 in C sharp minor (opus 27 no 2, nick-named 'Moonlight'), no 21 in C major ('Waldstein', opus 53), no 23 in F minor ('Appassionata', opus 57), no 29 in B flat ('Hammerklavier', opus 106); also for the piano, the 'Diabelli' Variations (opus 120); and many other instrumental works.

Bix Beiderbecke

Beiderbecke, Leon Bismarck 'Bix' (1903–31).

American cornet player and one of the first great white jazz musicians. He played in several bands, including the Wolverines, and later with the Paul Whiteman band, winning acclaim for his flawless technique and lilting style. He also wrote a piano piece, 'In a Mist', which is notable for its Debussy-like harmonies.

Bellini, Vincenzo (1801–35).

Italian composer of operas in the *bel canto* style, including *I Puritani* ('The Puritans'), *La Sonnambula* ('The Sleepwalker') and *Norma* (a Druidic priestess in Roman Gaul).

Berg, Alban (1885–1935).

Austrian composer. He was a pupil of Schoenberg and developed twelve-tone methods of composition in his own work, proving that they could be the basis for very expressive and beautiful music. He is best known today for his opera *Wozzeck* (about a poor, persecuted soldier) and his Violin Concerto (written on the death of a friend's daughter and bearing the dedication 'in memory of an angel').

Berlin, Irving (born 1888). American song-writer, the son of Russian immigrants, whose real name was Israel Baline. His famous songs, many written for stage shows or films, include 'Alexander's Ragtime Band', 'I'm Dreaming of a White Christmas' and 'How Deep is the Ocean?'. He also wrote the music for the stage and film musical *Call me Madam*, and the patriotic song 'God Bless America'. He never learnt properly how to play the piano or read music.

Berlioz, Hector (1803–69). French composer and major figure in the development of Romantic music. He studied music against his father's wishes, and from his days as a student in Paris had to struggle for his live-lihood, never earning the recognition or the rewards he thought he deserved. The two principal features of his music are vivid orchestration (he wrote a book on the subject) and compositions on a very large scale (inspired by the great open-air cere-monies of the French Revolutionary period), though he could write with delicacy and restraint. His works include the *Symphonie Fantastique*; the symphony *Harold in Italy* (based on a poem by Byron and with a part for solo viola, originally intended for Paganini); the dramatic symphony for soloists, chorus and orchestra *Romeo and Juliet* (after Shakespeare); the dramatic cantata, sometimes staged as an opera, *La Damnation de Faust* (after Goethe); the oratorio *L'Enfance du Christ* ('Childhood of Christ'); a Requiem Mass; song-cycle, with orchestra, *Nuits d'Ete* ('Summer Nights'); and the concert

overtures *Le Corsair* and *Le Carnaval Romain* (music taken from his opera *Benvenuto Cellini*). His greatest work for the stage, the opera *Les Troyens* ('The Trojans'), was never performed complete in his lifetime.

Bernart de Ventadorn (about 1130–95). One of the most famous of the troubadour poet-musicians of medieval Provence. He was much admired by Eleanor of Aquitaine, who invited him to England after her marriage to Henry II.

Bernstein, Leonard (born 1918). American conductor (closely asso-ciated with the New York Phil-harmonic Orchestra), pianist, and composer of the symphonies called *Jeremiah* and *Age of Anxiety*. In a lighter, often jazz-inspired style he has also written the music to the ballet *Fancy Free* (later adapted for the film *On The Town*) and to the very successful stage and film musical *West Side Story* (which retells the story of *Romeo and Juliet* in a New York City setting). A very unusual work is his *Mass* for singers, players and dancers.

Leonard Bernstein

Binchois, Gilles (about 1400–60). Burgundian soldier, priest and chief composer at the court of Philip the Good in Dijon, best remembered today for his secular *chansons* (songs), often very expressive for their time.

Bizet, Georges (1838–75). French composer with a wonderful natural gift for melody and strong, bright orchestration, as heard in the incidental music he wrote to Daudet's play *L'Arlésienne* ('The Girl from Arles') and the suite *Jeux d'enfants* ('Children's Games'). He also wrote the operas *The Pearl Fishers* and *The Fair Maid of Perth* (based on the novel by Sir Walter Scott). His last opera, *Carmen* (the name of the Spanish gipsy heroine), has long been one of the most popular in the repertory. Tragically, Bizet died soon after the première, just before it became a real success. A Symphony in C, written when Bizet was only seventeen, is also a very popular piece of concert music.

Bliss, Sir Arthur (1891–1975). Master of the Queen's Music and composer of several works with interesting and unusual associations, notably the 'Colour' Symphony (which relates the mood of each movement to a particular colour) and the ballet *Checkmate* (based on a game of chess); also of music to the film *Things to Come*.

Bloch, Ernest (1880–1959). Swiss-born composer who settled in the United States, becoming an American citizen. His best-known pieces are those inspired by Jewish history and religion. They include the 'Israel' Symphony for voices and orchestra; *Avodath Hakodesh* ('Sacred Service') for baritone, chorus and orchestra; *Shelomo* ('Solomon') for cello and orchestra; and *Baal Shem* (the name of a seventeenth-century Hebrew leader) for violin and piano.

Boccherini, Luigi (1743–1805). Italian composer and cellist. He wrote symphonies, concertos and over 200 string quintets and quartets, similar in style and character to the music of his contemporary Haydn, but remembered today largely on the strength of a single minuet.

Borodin, Alexander (1833–87). Russian composer and member of the group of nationalist composers known as 'The Five'. He was also an eminent chemist and could spare little time for music. Some of the music he did write has become very popular, including the 'Polovtsian Dances' from his opera *Prince Igor* (completed by his colleague Rimsky-Korsakov); the symphonic poem *In the Steppes of Central Asia*; also two completed symphonies.

Boulez, Pierre (born 1925). French composer and conductor. As a composer he has developed Schoenberg's twelve-tone methods of composition, often applying mathematical principles to his work, and his music is considered to be 'advanced' in character. As a conductor he has also specialized in the music of Schoenberg and other twelve-tone composers, though he has won acclaim for his interpretations of Wagner, Debussy and Stravinsky. He is Director of the Centre for Acoustical Studies in Paris.

Boyce, William (1710–79). English organist and composer of stage music and songs, including the well-known patriotic song 'Heart of Oak', also of several symphonies in the early Classical style.

Brahms, Johannes (1833–97). German composer. He was born in Hamburg and as a young man received much help and encouragement from Robert and Clara Schumann. After Robert's death, Clara remained one of his very few close friends. Like Beethoven before him, he settled in Vienna, where he died. Although a fine pianist, Brahms gave most of his time to composition, combining Classical forms like the symphony and sonata with a more Romantic mood. His early works are generally large and serious in character, his later ones are far more relaxed, warm and mellow in spirit, and often of great harmonic and rhythmic subtlety. His output includes four symphonies—no 1 in C minor, no 2 in D major, no 3 in F major, no 4 in E minor; two piano concertos—no 2 in B flat being one of the grandest of all concertos, with four instead of the usual three movements; a violin concerto; a 'double' concerto for violin and cello; the orchestral Variations on the St Anthony Chorale (formerly thought to be a theme by Haydn); the *Academic Festival* and *Tragic* concert overtures; the choral *Ein deutsches Requiem* ('A German Requiem', based not on the Catholic Requiem Mass but on selected passages from the Lutheran Bible); sonatas and other instrumental chamber music works, notably three string quartets; many piano pieces and *Lieder* (Songs); also the popular Hungarian Dances.

Britten, Benjamin (1913–76). English composer mainly of stage and vocal music, written in a fairly traditional but distinctive style that has had a wide appeal. His works include the operas *Peter Grimes* (based on a poem by George Crabbe and set on the Suffolk coast); *Billy Budd* (about the British navy of Nelson's time); *The Turn of the Screw* (after the ghost story by Henry James) and *Death in Venice* (based on the novel by Thomas Mann); 'Spring' Symphony for voices and orchestra (ending with 'Sumer is icumen in'); Variations and Fugue on a Theme of Purcell (*The Young Person's Guide to the Orchestra*); *Let's Make an Opera* and other works for children. Britten also founded the Aldeburgh Music Festival on the Suffolk coast, not far from his birthplace.

Benjamin Britten

Bruch, Max (1838–1920).
German composer of operas, symphonies and other orchestral works—notably the Violin Concerto no 1 in G minor—written in a generally Romantic style.

Bruckner, Anton (1824–96).
Austrian organist and composer. His principal works are nine symphonies, whose rich orchestration and grand scale reflect his great love of Wagner's music—no 3 is dedicated to him, while Symphonies nos 7, 8 and 9 contain parts for the Wagner tuba; no 4 is named the 'Romantic'. An interesting oddity is an early symphony which is known as Symphony no 0. Bruckner, a devout Catholic, also composed three masses, a Requiem and a *Te Deum* (hymn of thanksgiving).

Bull, John (1563–1628).
English composer and organist, but specially noted today for his keyboard pieces for the virginals, one of which is thought to be the origin of 'God Save the Queen'.

Bülow, Hans Guido von (1830–94).
German pianist and conductor—one of the first to make his name primarily as a conductor on account of his exciting interpretations and concert-hall manner. He worked closely with Wagner for some years, and his wife Cosima (Liszt's daughter) left him for the composer.

Buxtehude, Diderik (1637–1707).
Danish organist and composer who worked for most of his life in Germany, so that he is better known as Dietrich Buxtehude. His playing and his organ music influenced Bach (who once walked nearly 200 miles to hear him play). Handel also visited him and admired his music.

Byrd, William (1543–1623).
English organist and composer who lived during the troubled religious times that led to the creation of the Church of England. Though a Catholic, he wrote music both for his own and for the Anglican Church; also renowned for his madrigals, keyboard pieces and other secular music. He and his older colleague Thomas Tallis were given a monopoly of music printing (then a new technique) by Elizabeth I.

Below: William Byrd

Anton Bruckner

Cage, John (born 1912).
American composer and important figure in twentieth-century musical thought. His idea of the 'Prepared Piano'—using objects placed between or over the strings— produced a startling new range of sounds. He also conceived of an extraordinary piece called *4'33"* (4 min 33 sec), during which time a pianist sits before a piano and makes certain gestures but does not play a single note. The idea is to draw the audience's attention to the multitude of sounds that still exist during periods of apparent silence.

Callas, Maria (1923–77).
Greek-American operatic soprano, whose original name was Kalogeropoulou. She was acclaimed especially for her singing of Italian opera—

Bellini, Donizetti, Puccini—and for her very powerful stage presence.

Carissimi, Giacomo (1605–74).
Italian composer, important in musical history for his pioneer work in the field of oratorio. *Jephtha*, his most famous oratorio, served as a model for later composers.

Carter, Elliott (born 1908).
American composer who has been influenced by the so-called neo-Classical style of Stravinsky, and has also used serial methods of composition related to the twelve-tone techniques of Schoenberg. His works include the ballet *Minotaur* and a symphony.

Below: Enrico Caruso

Caruso, Enrico (1873–1921).
Italian operatic tenor who was one of the first serious musical artists to become a recording star (in the early days of acoustical recording) and achieved world-wide fame as a result.

Casals, Pau (1876–1973).
Spanish cellist, noted especially for his playing of Bach's music for unaccompanied cello, which he did much to revive. He held strong political views, exiling himself from Spain after Franco's victory in the Civil War, and founding the Prades music festival in southern France. As a Catalan nationalist he preferred the first name Pau to the Spanish Pablo.

Cavalli, Pietro Francesco (1620–76).
Italian composer who worked with Monteverdi in Venice for some time and wrote more than thirty operas of his own.

Chabrier, Emmanuel (1841–94).
French pianist, conductor and composer. His rhapsody *España*, inspired by a visit to Spain, is a favourite orchestral showpiece, and exuberant in spirit like much of his other music, though later in life he suffered badly from depression.

Chaliapin, Feodor Ivanovich (1875–1938).
Russian operatic bass, noted above all for his moving performances of the title role in Mussorgsky's opera *Boris Godunov*.

Charpentier, Marc-Antoine (about 1634–1704)
French composer of church music, also of operas and ballets. Like Lully, he worked with Molière and other dramatists of the time.

Chávez, Carlos (born 1899)
Mexican composer who has studied his country's folk music and developed a national style. One of his works includes native Mexican instruments and is named after the Aztec god of music.

Luigi Cherubini

Cherubini, Luigi (1760–1842).

Italian composer who worked for most of his life in Paris, where he was director of the Conservatory and one of the most eminent musical figures of his time. He wrote several successful operas, and Beethoven greatly admired his work. Today, the only piece of his music which is widely known is the overture to his opera *Iphigénie en Aulide*.

Chopin, Frédéric Francois (1810–49).

Polish-French composer and pianist. He was born in Poland, and though he spent most of his adult life in Paris remained intensely patriotic towards the country of his birth. Chopin composed almost exclusively for the piano. His music is often Romantically expressive, but always beautifully fashioned and refined, and marvellously suited to his chosen instrument. He wrote two early piano concertos, primarily for his own use on concert tours, and three sonatas; otherwise his output consists of groups of fairly short individual pieces—polonaises and mazurkas (based on traditional types of Polish dance), studies (*études*) which highlight different aspects of piano technique, preludes, ballades, waltzes, scherzos, impromptus and nocturnes. Some of these pieces have been given fanciful nicknames, not by Chopin, e.g. the 'Revolutionary' and 'Winter Wind' studies, the 'Raindrop' Prelude, 'Minute' Waltz. The ballet *Les Sylphides* is based on his music. Chopin is also famous for his love affair with George Sand, assumed name of the writer Aurore Dudevant. He died of consumption like many others in the past.

Cimarosa, Domenico (1749–1801).

Italian composer of over sixty operas, including *Il Matrimonio segreto* ('The Secret Marriage'), a comic opera similar in style to some of Mozart's. Cimarosa was a very successful man, holding important posts in Vienna and St Petersburg.

Clementi, Muzio (1752–1832).

Italian pianist and composer. He was a pioneer composer of piano music, including a collection of studies called *Gradus ad Parnassum* ('Steps to Parnassus'—the mountain which in Greek mythology was the home of the Muses). He settled in London where he also manufactured pianos.

Coleridge-Taylor, Samuel (1875–1912).

English composer—though his father was West African—of several musically picturesque works, notably a group of cantatas collectively called *Hiawatha*, inspired by Longfellow's poem of Red Indian life.

Copland, Aaron (born 1900).

American composer who has done much for the cause of his country's music by basing many of his own compositions on American folk songs and dances, also jazz, or on scenes from American life. His works include the ballets *Billy the Kid, Rodeo* and *Appalachian Spring*, the orchestral piece *El Salón México*, and *A Lincoln Portrait* for narrator and orchestra. He has also written symphonies, a clarinet concerto specially for Benny Goodman, and some music for films.

Corelli, Arcangelo (1653–1713).

Italian composer and violinist. He was one of the first great composers of music for the violin family of instruments, doing much to establish the concerto grosso form of writing for strings. Handel was greatly influenced by his style.

Above: Aaron Copland

Left: François Couperin

Couperin, François (1668–1733).
French composer, harpsichordist and
organist, sometimes called Couperin
le grand ('the Great') to distinguish
him from other members of his very
musical family. He served at the court
of Louis XIV, writing many organ
and choral works for use in church;
but is best remembered for his
harpsichord compositions, mostly
written in groups called *ordres* or
suites (some with picturesque titles)
which are among the finest
instrumental pieces of the Baroque
period. He wrote a book on
keyboard technique, now a valuable
guide to the playing styles of his
time.

Czerny, Carl (1791–1857).
Austrian composer, and key figure in
the history of piano music. He took
lessons from Beethoven, was, in turn,
a teacher of Liszt, and wrote a large
number of studies for the instrument.

Dallapiccola, Luigi (1904–75).
Italian composer who followed
Schoenberg's twelve-tone methods
of composition, seeking to extend the
appreciation of such music in a wide
range of compositions, including
operas, piano pieces and songs.

Davis, Miles (born 1926).
American jazz trumpeter who
developed, during the 1950s, a very
'cool' ethereal style, completely
different from the energetic style of
more traditional jazz.

Debussy, Claude-Achille
(1862–1918).
French composer. He was born at St
Germain-en-Laye, not far from Paris,
and lived in that city most of his life.
Debussy's music owes something in
spirit both to the work of the
Impressionist painters and to the
group of French poets called the
Symbolists. His own harmonic style,
which he developed slowly and
carefully, is one of the most original
in music, and his influence on
twentieth-century music has been
great. His principal works for
orchestra are *Prélude à l'après-midi
d'un faune* ('Prelude to the Afternoon
of a Faun'); *Nocturnes*; *La Mer* ('The
Sea'); *Images*, including *Ibéria*
('Spain'); and music for the ballet
Jeux. He wrote one opera, *Pelléas et
Mélisande*. His best-known piano
works are the *Suite Bergamasque*,
which includes 'Clair de lune'
('Moonlight'); *Estampes* ('Prints'),
including 'Jardins sous la pluie'
('Gardens in the Rain'); two sets of
Images; two more substantial sets of
preludes, including 'La Fille aux
cheveux de lin' ('The Girl with the
Flaxen Hair'), 'La Cathédrale
engloutie' ('The Sunken Cathedral')
and 'Feux d'artifice' ('Fireworks');
the suite *Children's Corner*, including
'Golliwog's Cakewalk'; and twelve
studies (*études*). He also composed
some important groups of *chansons*
(songs), and some instrumental
works, including a string quartet.

Above: Claude-Achille Debussy

Right: A very late portrait of Frederick
Delius. Blind and paralysed, he dictated
his last compositions to Eric Fenby, a
younger English composer.

Delibes, Léo (1836–91). French composer of operas and songs, but best known today for his tuneful and brightly orchestrated music to the ballets *Coppélia* and *Sylvia*.

Delius, Frederick (1862–1934). English composer, although his family was of German descent and he spent most of his life abroad. He developed a style which owed something to Grieg but was unmistakably his own—noted for its 'fluid' and shifting harmonies. His best-known works are the descriptive orchestral pieces *On Hearing the First Cuckoo in Spring, Summer Night on the River, The Walk to the Paradise Garden* (from the opera *A Village Romeo and Juliet*), and the 'English Rhapsody' *Brigg Fair* (a set of variations on a Lincolnshire folk song). But Delius also wrote some large choral and orchestral works, notably *A Mass of Life* (based on the writings of the German philosopher Nietzsche), which express his strong mystical feelings about Nature.

Donizetti, Gaetano (1797–1848). Italian composer of operas in the *bel canto* style, both serious (*Lucia di Lammermoor*, based on a novel by Sir Walter Scott) and comic (*Don Pasquale* and *La Fille du régiment*, composed for the Paris Opera).

Dowland, John (1563–1626). English lutenist and composer who served the king of Denmark for some years, and latterly Charles I of England. His ayres and many compositions or arrangements for the lute are both beautifully expressive and landmarks in the history of song and of instrumental music.

Dufay, Gillaume (about 1400–74). Netherlands composer who served both the Pope and the Burgundian court during his long and illustrious life. He wrote church masses and secular *chansons* (songs), and among his pupils was the great Jean de Ockeghem.

Dukas, Paul (1865–1935). French composer and scholar of old music. His own works, influenced by the musical 'impressionism' of Debussy, Ravel and other contemporary figures, include the well-known *L'Apprenti Sorcier* ('The Sorcerer's Apprentice'), an orchestral piece describing how the apprentice dabbles in his master's magic with disastrous results, but the sorcerer returns home in time to save the day.

Dunstable, John (about 1390–1453). English composer, mathematician and astrologer who for many years served the Duke of Bedford, Regent of France and brother of Henry V of England. His songs, church masses and motets were greatly admired throughout Western Europe during his lifetime and influenced the music of Binchois, Dufay and others who worked at the court of Burgundy.

Duparc, Henri (1848–1933). French composer whose output was very small due to a severe mental breakdown. However, he is remembered for a small and very fine group of *chansons* (songs).

Gaetano Donizetti

Antonin Dvořák

Sir Edward Elgar

Dvořák, Antonin (1841–1904). Bohemian-born composer who, with Smetana, worked for Czech national independence; and from humble beginnings became one of the most famous men of his time, crowning his career with an extended visit to the United States. He wrote in almost every musical form of the period, combining something of the style of Brahms (who was his friend) with elements of Bohemian folk song and dance. His works include: nine symphonies—no 9 in E minor, subtitled 'From the New World', being partly inspired by Negro folk songs; the Cello Concerto in B minor; the opera *Rusalka* (named after a water spirit from Slavonic legend); symphonic poems; string quartets and other chamber music compositions; and the popular Slavonic Dances and Slavonic Rhapsodies.

Elgar, Sir Edward (1857–1934). English composer, born near Worcester, who is generally regarded as the greatest since Purcell, and the one who opened the way for other English composers of this century. The work that first won him recognition after years of neglect was the 'Enigma' Variations (full title— Variations on an Original Theme for Orchestra—each variation being a musical portrait of one of his friends). Other important compositions, often written in a rich and vivid style, are: the oratorio *The Dream of Gerontius*; two symphonies; a violin and a cello concerto; the 'symphonic study' *Falstaff* (after the Shakespearian character); and the concert overture *Cockaigne* (an evocation of the spirit of Edwardian London). The main theme from one of his 'Pomp and Circumstance' marches was made into the patriotic hymn 'Land of Hope and Glory', which Elgar came to detest.

Manuel de Falla

Gabriel Fauré

Ellington, Edward Kennedy 'Duke' (1899–1974).
American jazz musician and band leader. 'Duke' Ellington was a major figure in the world of jazz for nearly fifty years, employing some of the other most talented jazz musicians of his time and featuring arrangements and compositions noted for their subtle harmonies and instrumental 'colouring'. Pieces specially associated with him are 'Take the A Train', 'Satin Doll' and 'Cotton Tail'. A later record album, *Such Sweet Thunder*, was inspired by characters from Shakespeare.

Falla, Manuel de (1876–1946).
Spanish pianist and composer. He was born in the southern province of Andalusia, home of flamenco singing and dancing, and the melodies and rhythms of this music run through nearly everything he wrote. This strong feature of his music, and its popular appeal, made him the leading member of the Spanish nationalist group of composers. His principal

works are: the opera *La vida breve* ('Life is Short'); the ballets *El amor brujo* ('Love, the Magician', which includes the 'Ritual Fire Dance') and *The Three-Cornered Hat*; *Nights in the Gardens of Spain* for piano and orchestra; and Seven Popular Spanish Songs for soprano. Another unusual but beautiful piece is *Master Peter's Puppet Show*, a kind of miniature opera using marionettes.

Fauré, Gabriel (1845–1924).
French composer, organist and teacher. His refined style and often subtle harmonies influenced his younger French contemporaries, including Ravel. His most significant compositions were his groups of *chansons* (songs), but he also wrote a beautiful setting of the Requiem Mass, incidental music to Maeterlinck's play *Pelléas et Mélisande* (which Debussy turned into an opera), and many chamber-music works and piano pieces. His Pavane for orchestra and chorus is a very popular concert piece.

Field, John (1782–1837).
Irish pianist and composer. He worked with Clementi in his piano-manufacturing business, then settled in St Petersburg (now Leningrad), winning great fame as a pianist on concert tours. He wrote piano concertos and a number of shorter piano pieces called nocturnes which served as a model for Chopin.

Flagstad, Kirsten Marie (1895–1962).
Norwegian operatic soprano, famous for her Wagnerian roles and above all for her singing of Brünnhilde in *Der Ring des Nibelungen*.

Foster, Stephen Collins (1826–64).
American composer of such famous 'drawing-room' ballads as 'Jeannie with the Light Brown Hair', and songs like 'My Old Kentucky Home' and 'Camptown Races' which were tremendously popular around the turn of the century with 'nigger' minstrel shows (supposed to be a style of black man's entertainment).

César Franck

Wilhelm Furtwängler

George Gershwin

Franck, César (1822–90).
Belgian composer. In his own
lifetime he was famous as an organist
in Paris, contributing much to the
great tradition of French organ
music; also a much-loved teacher at
the Paris Conservatory. Today he is
best known for his Symphony in D
minor and Symphonic Variations for
piano and orchestra, written in a rich
harmonic style noted for its
'chromaticism'.

**Frederick II ('The Great') of
Prussia** (1712–86).
He was a great patron of music.
J.S.Bach's *Musical Offering* was
written for him, and he also
employed Bach's son Carl Philipp
Emanuel. He was himself a keen
flautist and composed much music
for the flute.

Frescobaldi, Girolamo
(1583–1643).
Italian composer and in his own time
a very famous organist, whose many
compositions for organ and
harpsichord—toccatas and fugues—

had a big influence on the music of
others, especially in Germany.

Furtwängler, Wilhelm
(1886–1954).
German conductor associated chiefly
with the Berlin and Vienna
Philharmonic orchestras and
remembered for the power and
intensity of his interpretations of
Beethoven, Wagner and Bruckner.

Gabrieli, Andrea (about 1510–86).
and his nephew **Giovanni**
(1557–1612).
Italian composers, both organists at St
Mark's Basilica, Venice, who created
a very dramatic 'antiphonal' style of
church music for groups of voices
and instrumentalists, very similar in
effect to modern stereophonic
reproduction. Such grand and
dramatic music also symbolized the
wealth and power of Venice in
Renaissance times.

Geminiani, Francesco
(1687–1762).
Italian violinist and composer. He

was a pupil of Corelli and another big
figure in the development of the
concerto grosso for the violin family
of instruments. He also wrote an
important treatise on the violin.

Gershwin, George (1898–1937).
American song-writer and composer,
of Russian immigrant parents (born
Jacob Gershovitz). Starting his career
in Tin Pan Alley, traditional music-
publishing quarter of New York
City, he went on to write (often to
his brother Ira's lyrics) some of the
most famous songs of the 1920s and
1930s—'Fascinating Rhythm', 'The
Man I Love', 'Our Love is Here to
Stay'. Then for band leader Paul
Whiteman he composed the
Rhapsody in Blue for piano and
orchestra, combining jazz and Latin
American features with more
'symphonic' forms. Later works in
this style are the Piano Concerto in F,
the symphonic poem *An American in
Paris* and the all-Negro opera *Porgy
and Bess* (containing some of his finest
songs—'Summertime', 'Bess, you is
my woman now').

Gesualdo, Carlo

(about 1560–1615).
Italian prince, lutenist and composer of some madrigals noted for their expressive and adventurous harmonies. He is also remembered as the murderer of his wife and her lover.

Gibbons, Orlando (1583–1625).

English organist, virginalist and composer of church music and some very expressive madrigals (including 'The Silver Swan'). He also contributed some keyboard pieces to a famous early printed edition called *Parthenia*.

Gieseking, Walter (1895–1956).

German pianist who specialized in French music, notably that of Debussy.

Gigli, Beniamino (1890–1957).

Italian operatic tenor, internationally famous especially for his singing of Verdi and Puccini.

Glazunov, Alexander

(1865–1936).
Russian composer of symphonies, concertos, ballets (including *The Seasons*) and piano music in a conservative, Romantic style and less nationalistic in character than the music of most of his Russian colleagues.

Glinka, Mikhail Ivanovich

(1804–57).
He is often called the 'father of Russian music', since he was the first Russian composer to become widely known both at home and abroad; and his example was a tremendous encouragement to later Russian nationalist composers. Glinka's best-known works are the operas *Ivan Susanin* (originally produced as *A Life for the Tsar*) and *Ruslan and Ludmilla* (the overture to which is a concert favourite).

Gluck, Christoph Willibald

(1714–87).
German composer who visited London and worked mainly in Paris and Vienna. He was a great reforming figure in the history of opera, arguing that music in opera should serve the dramatic action and not ruin it for the sake of convention or the reputation of star singers. These ideas were taken up in different ways by Mozart, Beethoven, Wagner and others. His own operas, mostly based on plays or stories from Classical antiquity, include *Orfeo ed Euridice*, *Alceste* (to which he wrote a famous preface presenting his ideas), *Iphigénie en Tauride* and *Armide*. He also wrote some instrumental music.

Mikhail Glinka

Benny Goodman

Charles Gounod when aged twenty-one.

Goodman, Benny (born 1909).
American jazz clarinettist and band leader who formed some of the most exciting jazz-swing bands of the 1930s and 1940s and was known as the 'King of Swing'. As a highly gifted soloist he also played the clarinet music of Mozart and Weber and commissioned pieces from Hindemith, Bartók and Copland.

Gounod, Charles (1818–93).
French composer of symphonies, oratorios, much church music and, above all, operas, who was also one of the most successful and famous musicians of his age. The ballet music from his opera *Faust* is still widely known, and sometimes the opera itself is still produced, but most of his other music has now gone out of fashion.

Grainger, Percy Aldridge
(1882–1961).
Australian-born pianist and composer who lived in England for some years before settling in the United States and becoming an American citizen. He collected and edited British folk music, making a special arrangement of the traditional Irish tune known as the 'Londonderry Air'. His own compositions, light and breezy in style, include *Country Gardens* and *Handel in the Strand*.

Granados, Enrique
(1867–1916).
Spanish pianist and composer, and important member of the Spanish nationalist group of composers. His set of piano pieces called *Goyescas* were inspired by the paintings of his fellow-countryman Francisco Goya, and contain the well-known *The Maiden and the Nightingale*. These *Goyescas* also formed the basis of an opera. Granados was a tragic victim of war, when the ship on which he was returning from America was torpedoed and sunk.

Grieg, Edvard Hagerup
(1843–1907).
Norwegian composer who developed a distinctive nationalist style based on the folk songs and dances of his native land, and was much honoured both at home and abroad. He is sometimes called a 'miniaturist' because apart from his very popular Piano Concerto in A minor he wrote no large-scale orchestral or choral works and no operas. But his compositions, including the extensive incidental music he wrote for Ibsen's play *Peer Gynt* and the *Holberg Suite*, are always most skilfully constructed and harmonized.

Guido d'Arezzo (about 995–1050).
Italian monk and important figure in the development of musical notation and theory. He is chiefly remembered as the originator of a method of learning music on which the modern Tonic Sol-Fa system is based. He also devised a method of teaching music to choirs called the 'Guidonian Hand', using sections of the fingers to represent different notes.

Handel, George Frideric
(1685–1759).
German-born composer (originally named Georg Friedrich Händel) who settled in London and became a British subject. His life fluctuated between periods of great success and others of failure and hardship, largely because he chose to run his own affairs rather than seek the patronage of church or state. At first he devoted his time largely to opera, composing in rapid succession a number of such works in the fashionable Italian *opera seria* style. Among these are *Rinaldo*, *Berenice* (still famous for its overture), *Julius Caesar*, *Orlando* and *Xerxes* (from which comes the aria known as 'Handel's Largo'). When this type of opera went out of fashion, and after recovery from illness, Handel turned his attention more to oratorio, composing such works as *Saul, Israel in Egypt, Judas Maccabeus, Solomon*

(including 'Arrival of the Queen of Sheba') and, above all, *Messiah* (containing the 'Hallelujah Chorus'). Handel also wrote much instrumental music, including *Music for the Royal Fireworks* and the *Water Music*, pieces in the concerto grosso form, organ concertos (originally often played by Handel himself during the intervals of oratorio performances), sonatas for various instruments, and the well-known set of harpsichord variations nicknamed, but not by the composer, 'The Harmonious Blacksmith'. Handel's robust style of Baroque music has remained very popular in English-speaking countries. It has also been much admired by other great composers. Beethoven said, 'When Handel chooses, he can strike like a thunderbolt!'

Harris, Roy Ellsworth (born 1898).
Eminent American composer and teacher. He has made use of American folk song and dance, but re-creating it in an up-to-date style that gives much of his music a strong spacious sound. His compositions include symphonies, concertos and chamber music.

Haydn, Franz Joseph (1732–1809).
Austrian composer of humble peasant origins who became musical director for many years at the court of the Esterházy family, and as a famous man made two highly successful visits to London. Haydn perfected the Classical forms of the symphony, string quartet and keyboard sonata, thus laying the foundations for Beethoven, Brahms and other great symphonic composers who followed him. He is officially credited with 104 symphonies, of which the last twelve were specially written for London and are known collectively as the 'Salomon Symphonies' after the violinist Johann Peter Salomon, who organized the composer's visits. Many of the symphonies have nicknames, with or without some reason, such as 'Farewell', 'Bear',

'Surprise', 'Clock', 'Miracle', 'Drumroll', 'Military'. Of his eighty string quartets, the so-called 'Emperor' Quartet is the most famous because it contains the melody which later became the national anthem first of the Austrian Empire and today of the German Federal Republic. Haydn also wrote operas and masses, mostly for the court at Esterházy, and towards the end of his life two oratorios, *The Creation* and *The Seasons*. His brother Michael (1737–1806) was *Kapellmeister* to the Archbishop of Salzburg and a composer mainly of church music.

Heifetz, Jascha (born 1901).
Russian-born violinist who settled in the United States and adopted American nationality. He won international fame and commissioned concertos from several composers, including Walton.

Henze, Hans Werner (born 1926).
German composer who has used twelve-tone methods of composition, and also written some music for jazz band and symphony orchestra. Several of his stage works have made a big impression, including the opera *Elegy for Young Lovers* (based on an English libretto by W.H. Auden) and the dramatic oratorio *The Raft of the Medusa*, inspired by Géricault's famous painting, and dedicated to the revolutionary leader Che Guevara.

Herman, Woodrow Wilson, 'Woody' (born 1913).
American jazz clarinettist and leader of a series of famous jazz-swing bands usually called the 'Herman Herd'. His own playing inspired Stravinsky to write his 'Ebony' Concerto ('ebony stick' being a slang name for a clarinet).

Hindemith, Paul (1895–1963).
German violinist, viola-player and composer who eventually settled in the United States after the Nazis came to power. He composed a good

deal of what is called *Gebrauchsmusik* ('Utility Music'), meaning music intended to be an everyday part of people's lives rather than more elevated 'art' music. Two of his other works remain popular in the concert hall: the symphony *Mathis der Maler* (based on music taken from his opera about the German Renaissance painter Matthias Grünewald), and the *Symphonic Metamorphoses on Themes of Weber*, the rather severe title for some very entertaining music.

Holiday, Billie (1915–59).
Jazz vocalist recognized as one of the greatest interpreters of Blues and Blues-style music. For about twenty years she sang with many of the finest jazz instrumentalists, but as with many other talented and sensitive jazz musicians the pressures of her way of life destroyed her career and led to her premature death.

Holst, Gustav (1874–1934).
English composer of Swedish descent, also a noted teacher. His orchestral suite *The Planets*—in which the astrological character of each of the individual planets is portrayed in turn—combines his inspired orchestration and highly distinctive harmonic style with his deep interest in mysticism. Other works are the equally mystical *Hymn of Jesus* for chorus and orchestra, the opera *The Perfect Fool*, and the symphonic poem *Egdon Heath*.

Honegger, Arthur (1892–1955).
Swiss composer, but born in France and one of the French group of composers known as 'Les Six'. Like the others of this group, he soon branched out creatively on his own, his works including the oratorio *King David* and music to the play *Joan of Arc at the Stake*. Another piece, at one time very well known, was his orchestral *Pacific 231*, conveying the sound and motion of a steam railway locomotive.

Gustav Holst

Leoš Janáček

Horowitz, Vladimir (born 1904). Russian-born pianist who settled in the United States and earned the highest reputation for his dazzling technique. Illness terminated his concert career in 1950. He is married to Toscanini's daughter Wanda.

Hovhaness, Alan (born 1911). American conductor, organist and composer. His family were Armenian, and his own compositions have been much influenced by Asiatic and Middle Eastern music. One of these is the concerto for piano and strings with the Armenian title *Lousadzak* ('The Coming of Light'). Another interesting work is *And God Created Great Whales*, which uses the recorded sounds of a whale.

Hummel, Johann Nepomuk (1778–1837). Austrian pianist and composer, a pupil of Haydn, Mozart and Clementi, very famous in his own day as a performer, and composer of piano concertos and other piano works in an attractive blend of Classical and early Romantic styles.

Humperdinck, Engelbert (1854–1921). German composer, a close friend and colleague of Wagner, now chiefly remembered for his opera *Hansel and Gretel* (based on the one of the fairy tales of the brothers Grimm).

Ibert, Jacques (1890–1962). French composer, not a member of 'Les Six', but writing music in the same light, sometimes irreverent style. His works include the orchestral *Escales* ('Ports of Call') and *Divertissement*, and piano pieces such as 'Le petit âne blanc' ('The Little White Donkey').

Ireland, John (1879–1962). English composer whose music is generally written in a Romantic but quite personal style. His works include a piano concerto, the *London* concert overture and his well-known setting of John Masefield's poem 'Sea Fever'.

Ives, Charles (1874–1954). American composer who combined writing music with a successful business career. In fact, he was an astonishingly advanced and original musical thinker, though having very little contact with other more established composers of his time, such as Schoenberg and Bartók. His compositions, mostly inspired by places and events in his home territory of New England, include the orchestral *Three Places in New England* and the 'Concord' Piano Sonata.

Janáček, Leoš (1854–1928). Czech composer whose music is both strongly nationalistic in character and original in style, being based largely on the sound of the Czech language. This is particularly the case with his operas, *Jenůfa*, *Katya Kabanova*, *The Cunning Little Vixen* (which also reflects many sounds from nature), *The Makropoulos Affair* and *From the House of the Dead*. Other works include the *Glagolitic Mass* for chorus and orchestra (Glagolitic being an old Slav church language), the orchestral *Sinfonietta*, the symphonic poem *Taras Bulba*, and the String Quartet called *Intimate Letters*.

Joachim, Joseph (1831–1907).
Hungarian violinist and close friend
of Brahms who often consulted him
on technical matters and whose
Violin Concerto is dedicated to him.
However, Joachim was also a
composer in his own right, his works
including three violin concertos and
concert overtures.

Joplin, Scott (1868–1917).
American jazz pianist and composer.
The son of an ex-slave, Scott Joplin
hoped to transform ragtime and
other early jazz styles into concert
music, and when he failed to do this
sank into deep depression. Today he
is remembered for such charming
piano pieces as 'Maple Leaf Rag' and
'The Entertainer'. He also wrote an
opera.

Josquin des Prés
(about 1450–1521).
Netherlands composer who served
the Pope for some years and then the
French court. He was much revered
in his own time, notably by Luther.
Today we recognize him as one of
the key figures of Renaissance music,
bringing a new freshness and vigour
to choral music of all kinds in a style
known as *musica reservata*—a Latin
term probably meaning music
reserved for those with finer feelings.

Karajan, Herbert von (born 1908).
Austrian conductor closely associated
with the Berlin Philharmonic
Orchestra, the Vienna State Opera
and the Salzburg Easter Festival. He is
noted above all for the refined sound
and precision of his performances.

Kern, Jerome (1885–1945).
American song-writer who did most
to transform the European style of
operetta into the American stage and
film musical, his most celebrated
achievement in this field being *Show
Boat*. He also composed some works
for orchestra, including *Portrait of
Mark Twain*.

Zoltán Kodály

Khachaturian, Aram (1903–78).
Soviet Armenian composer who
made use of the folk music of his
homeland in many of his own works.
Among these is the ballet *Gayaneh*
containing the famous 'Sabre Dance'.

Kodály, Zoltán (1882–1967).
Hungarian composer who for some
time worked with his compatriot
Bartók in the field of folk music. This
shared interest has given their music
some points in common, although
Kodály soon developed his own
distinctive musical personality. His
compositions include the strongly
nationalistic *Psalmus Hungaricus* for
chorus and orchestra, the orchestral
Dances from Galanta and the
orchestral suite from his opera *Háry
János* which opens with a famous
musical 'sneeze', an indication,
according to Hungarian custom, that
the adventures of the folk hero Háry
János should not be taken too
seriously!

Korngold, Erich Wolfgang
(1897–1957).
Austrian-born composer who settled
in the United States and became an
American citizen. His works include
operas and concertos, but during the
1930s he moved to Hollywood and
specialized in writing film music.

Kreisler, Fritz (1875–1926).
Austrian violinist acclaimed for the
lyrical style of his playing. He also
composed some music, including a
number of violin pieces which he at
first credited to other dead composers,
including Gaetano Pugnani,
but then admitted to be his own.

Landino, Francesco
(about 1325–97).
Italian lutenist and composer, an
important representative of the *ars
nova* school of music and composer of
secular part-songs which led directly
to the development of the madrigal.
He was blind from childhood.

A young lady seated at a virginal, a painting by Johannes
Vermeer (1632–1675).

The Opera House, King's Haymarket, an aquatint coloured
by hand by Bluck after Rowlandson and Pugin, c. 1809.

Frederick, Prince of Wales, and his sisters painted by Philip
Mercier, 1733.

Lassus, Orlandus (1530–94).
Netherlands composer and one of the
most important figures of
Renaissance music. He was in great
demand as a choirmaster and director
of music, holding posts in Rome and
Antwerp and at the Bavarian court in
Munich, where he died. Lassus
composed more than 2000 choral and
vocal works—church masses and
motets, also many secular madrigals
—in the finest polyphonic style. He
is sometimes called by the Italian version of his name—Orlando di Lasso.

Lehár, Franz (1870–1948).
Hungarian composer of many
successful Viennese-style operettas,
notably *The Merry Widow*.

Leoncavallo, Ruggiero
(1858–1919).
Italian operatic composer. One of his
operas was a version of *La Bohème*,
but his only real success was *I
Pagliacci* ('The Clowns'), a story of
real-life drama among a group of
travelling players.

Léonin (about 1130–80).
French choirmaster of the so-called
Notre Dame School of Paris, and one
of the earliest people in Western
music to be known by name as a
composer. He compiled a *Great Book
of Organum* containing music for all
the main events of the church year.
Also sometimes known by the Latin
version of his name—Leoninus.

Lind, Jenny (1820–87).
Swedish soprano who attracted huge
audiences both in the United States
and in Britain and was one of the
highest-paid of all concert artists. She
was known as 'The Swedish
Nightingale'.

Liszt, Franz (or Ferencz)
(1811–86).
Hungarian pianist and composer.
Liszt was a major figure in
nineteenth-century music, first as a
tremendously successful concert
pianist, then, as musical director to

Franz Liszt

the court of Weimar, a serious composer, teacher and friend of many of
the other great musical figures of his
time. After a socially unconventional
life, including several famous love
affairs, he finally took holy orders in
the Roman Catholic Church, becoming known as the 'Abbé Liszt'.
He also held strong nationalist
feelings and at the end of his life
presided over the newly founded
Hungarian Academy of Music in
Budapest. As a composer Liszt made
important contributions to the field
of Romantic programme music. For
the orchestra he wrote the 'Faust'
Symphony (with a choral ending),
and in a number of other descriptive
orchestral works created the form of
the symphonic poem. For the piano
he composed some equally vivid
descriptive pieces, notably those
included in his albums called *Années
de Pèlerinage* ('Years of Pilgrimage').
In his Piano Sonata in B minor he
also introduced important new ideas
in musical structure and form; while
his Hungarian Rhapsodies and some
of his piano transcriptions of themes
from operas reflect his own
phenomenal pianistic technique. His
very popular 'Liebestraum' ('Dream
of Love') is a piano transcription of
one of his own songs.

Lully, Jean-Baptiste (1632–87).
French composer—actually born in
Italy as Giovanni Battista Lulli—
who rose to a position of great power
and importance at the court of Louis
XIV at Versailles. He created a brilliant new form of opera-ballet, and in
his overtures to these works influenced the development of Baroque
orchestral music. Lully also col-
laborated with some of the other
famous Frenchmen of his time,
including Molière. His end was most
unfortunate: he accidentally banged
his foot with his heavy conducting
staff and died of blood poisoning.

Luther, Martin (1483–1546).
German priest and monk and leader
of the Protestant Reformation, but
also a gifted musician. He introduced
a new form of church hymn called
the chorale. 'Ein feste Burg' ('A
Safe Stronghold is our God') is the
best-known of these, sometimes
called the Battle Hymn of the
Reformation. Later composers,
including J.S. Bach, quoted from
these chorales.

Macdowell, Edward (1861–1908).
American pianist and composer who
studied and then taught in Europe for
some years before returning to the
United States. He won much
popularity in his own lifetime, on
both sides of the Atlantic, on account
of his piano concertos and many
other shorter piano pieces, written in
an attractive Lisztian style. After his
death the Macdowell Colony in New
England was founded as a retreat for
other composers, writers and artists.

Machaut, Guillaume de
(about 1300–77).
French priest, poet and composer. He
was a leading member of the *ars nova*
school or style of music with his
settings of both religious and secular
texts, often composed in a very
elaborate polyphonic style. Among
his works is one of the earliest
surviving complete settings of the
church mass.

Gustav Mahler

Mahler, Gustav (1860–1911).
Austrian conductor and composer.
As a conductor, mainly of opera in
Vienna and New York, Mahler
demanded and obtained the highest
standards of performance. As a
composer he sometimes used his
music to convey his own inner
conflicts and anxieties, sometimes to
express great philosophical or
religious themes; while at the same
time he pointed the way to technical
advances in twentieth-century music
through his harmonies and
orchestration. His principal works are
nine completed symphonies (plus a
tenth recently completed from his
notes), all written for a very large
orchestra and generally long and
complex in construction. Nos 2
('Resurrection'), 3, 4 and 8 (the
'Symphony of a Thousand') also
require vocal soloists, a chorus, or
both. In addition, Mahler composed
several orchestral song-cycles,
including *Kindertotenlieder* ('Songs on
the Death of Children') and *Das Lied
von der Erde* ('The Song of the Earth').

Dame Nellie Melba

Martinů, Bohuslav (1890–1959).
Czech composer who lived in France
for some years and then settled in the
United States. He wrote operas,
symphonies, symphonic poems and
much instrumental music in a highly
personal but less nationalistic style
than that adopted by Smetana,
Dvořák, Janáček and other Czech
composers before him.

Mascagni, Pietro (1863–1945).
Italian operatic composer who, like
his near contemporary and fellow

countryman Leoncavallo, had just
one big success. This was *Cavalleria
Rusticana* ('Rustic Chivalry'), a
drama of Sicilian revenge and murder
in the realistic style of *verismo* opera.

Massenet, Jules (1842–1912).
French composer, mainly of operas
written in a clear, lyrical style.
Manon, based on the novel *Manon
Lescaut* by the Abbé Prévost which
Puccini also used, is Massenet's best-
known opera today. He also wrote
many songs.

Melba, Nellie (1861–1931).
Australian operatic soprano. She took
her professional name from her
birthplace—Melbourne—and was
one of the most fêted singers of her
age. Like Caruso, she added greatly
to her fame and reputation as one of
the earliest serious recording artists.

Mendelssohn-Bartholdy, Felix
(1809–47).
German conductor and composer,
usually just called Mendelssohn. He
was tremendously popular and
successful during his own lifetime
and for many years afterwards,
combining in his music Romantic
feeling with a restrained and Classical
sense of form. His best-known works
are: the truly magical overture to
Shakespeare's *A Midsummer Night's
Dream* (composed at the age of
seventeen), with other incidental
music to the play, including the
famous 'Wedding March', written
later; five symphonies–no 3 (the
'Scottish'), no 4 (the 'Italian'), no 5
(the 'Reformation'); the well-loved
Violin Concerto in E minor; the
concert overture *The Hebrides* (or
'Fingal's Cave', inspired by a visit to
the Western Isles of Scotland); much
chamber music, and several albums of
piano pieces called *Lieder ohne Worte*
('Songs Without Words', which
include such pieces as the so-called
'Bees' Wedding' and 'Spring Song').
As a conductor Mendelssohn was in
great demand both in Germany and
in Britain. It was specially for English
audiences, with their love of
Handelian oratorio, that he
composed his own oratorio *Elijah*.

Menotti, Gian-Carlo (born 1911).
Italian-born composer who has lived
and worked in the United States for
most of his life. His best-known
works are a series of operas, generally
written in a clear tuneful style and
some originally intended for television, including *Amelia Goes to the
Ball*, *The Medium*, *The Telephone*,
Amahl and the Night Visitors and *The
Saint of Bleecker Street*.

Yehudi Menuhin

Menuhin, Yehudi (born 1916).
American violinist whose boyhood fame included a remarkable association with Elgar, with whom he made some recordings. During his distinguished career Menuhin has commissioned works from such composers as Bartók, and helped to foster international goodwill with his work among young musicians of all nationalities. He also sometimes conducts.

Messiaen, Olivier (born 1908).
French composer whose most original style—almost a new musical 'language'—has been formed by his varied interests in such matters as religion and mysticism, the harmonic and rhythmic features of Indian music, and bird-song. He has written much organ music, notably *L'Ascension* and *La Nativité du Seigneur* ('The Birth of Our Lord'); piano works, including his *Catalogue d'Oiseaux* ('Catalogue of Birds'); and orchestral compositions, often with very exotic percussion effects, including the massive 'Turangalîla' Symphony (which also has a part for the electronic *Ondes Martenot*).

Meyerbeer, Jakob (or Giacomo) (1791–1864).
German composer who worked mainly in Paris, composing a series of operas, very popular in their day, noted for their spectacular themes and grandiose musical style. The most famous of them, *Les Huguenots*, deals with the massacre of French Protestant Huguenots.

Milhaud, Darius (1892–1974).
French composer and originally a member of the group of composers known as 'Les Six'. His output was considerable, much of it influenced by his interest in Latin American music and jazz. One of his best-known works of this kind is the ballet *La Création du monde* ('The Creation of the World').

Miller, Glenn (1904–44).
American dance band leader, immensely popular during the 1930s and 1940s on account of such famous swing numbers as 'In the Mood', 'Moonlight Serenade' and 'A String of Pearls'. As a US army officer he came to Britain with his band and was lost on a flight to France.

Monteverdi, Claudio (1567–1643).
Italian composer who held various court and church appointments, the last and most important of these being as director of music to the Basilica of St Mark, Venice. He wrote much fine and dramatic church music in the antiphonal style specially associated with St Mark's, also many madrigals, including some *madrigali spirituali* to religious words. Above all, Monteverdi is remembered as the first great composer of opera and also, because of his imaginative use of instruments in his operas, as a pioneer figure in the history of the orchestra. Many of his operas have been lost. Three that survive are *Orfeo*, *Il Ritorno d'Ulisse in Patria* ('The Return of Ulysses') and *L'Incoronazione di Poppea* ('The Coronation of Poppea', being based on events in the life of the Emperor Nero).

Morley, Thomas (1557–1603).
English organist and composer. A pupil of Byrd, Morley wrote music for the church, to both Latin and English texts, many instrumental pieces for the lute, viols and virginal, and some of the finest madrigals of the Elizabethan period (contributing to the famous madrigal collection called *The Triumphs of Oriana*). He almost certainly knew Shakespeare and composed songs for some of his plays, notably 'It was a Lover and his Lass' (in *As You Like It*). He also wrote an entertaining book called *Plaine and Easie Introduction to Practicall Musicke*.

Morton, Ferdinand 'Jelly Roll' (1885–1941).
American jazz pianist whose real name was Ferdinand Joseph La Menthe. He recorded some of his best music with a celebrated group called the 'Red Hot Peppers'. Years later he recorded reminiscences of his colourful life in New Orleans and examples of early jazz styles specially for the American Library of Congress.

Oliver Messiaen

Jakob Meyerbeer

Mozart, Wolfgang Amadeus
(1756–91).
Austrian composer. He was born in Salzburg and began life as a child prodigy, being taken round the courts of Europe by his father and winning much praise and fame. As a young man he held a post with the Archbishop of Salzburg, but when this ended he was largely thrown back on his own resources. He was in demand as a performer and composer and achieved great success with some of his operas, but did not have the temperament to manage his affairs or make his own way in the world and died in poverty, in Vienna. Much of Mozart's music is written in the charming eighteenth-century Rococo style, intended as social entertainment. His greatest music occurs in his operas or in those orchestral and instrumental works which combine mastery of Classical form with great expressive power and sometimes very advanced musical thinking. Mozart's principal operas are *Idomeneo*, *Die Entführung aus dem Serail* ('The Escape from the Harem', also known as *Il Seraglio*), *Le Nozze di Figaro* ('The Marriage of Figaro'), *Don Giovanni*, *Così fan tutte* (loosely translated as 'Women are all the same'), *Die Zauberflöte* ('The Magic Flute') and *La Clemenza di Tito* ('The Mercy of Titus'). His greatest orchestral and instrumental works include the symphonies no 36 in C major ('Linz' K425,), no 38 in D major ('Prague', K504), no 39 in E flat major (K543), no 40 in G minor (K550), and the last, no 41 in C major ('Jupiter', K551); the piano concertos in D minor (K466), in C minor (K491), and in C major (K503); the string quintets in C major (K515), in G minor (K516) and in D major (K593); and the six string quartets he dedicated to Haydn, including those in G major (K387), in D minor (K421), and in C major ('Dissonance', K465). His last commission was for a setting of the Requiem Mass (K626), which he morbidly believed he was writing for himself. In fact, he did die

Wolfgang Amadeus Mozart

before finishing the work, completed later by a pupil. Today Mozart's compositions are usually quoted with their 'K' number, after the scholar Ludwig von Köchel who catalogued and indexed them in their probable chronological order.

Mussorgsky, Modest (1839–81).
Russian composer and perhaps the most naturally gifted member of the group of nationalist composers known as 'The Five'. Mussorgsky was an army officer and later a civil servant; consequently his output of music was small, but of great originality. He composed some remarkable songs which share with Janáček's music a deep feeling for the rhythms and inflections of speech; the equally remarkable piano work *Pictures at an Exhibition* (prompted by a memorial exhibition of the work of an artist friend and later vividly orchestrated by Ravel); the symphonic poem *Night on the Bare Mountain*; and the opera *Boris Godunov*, based on events in Russian history. He died from drink leaving several other works unfinished.

Nicolai, Otto (1810–49).
German conductor, and composer of the opera *The Merry Wives of Windsor* (after the play by Shakespeare). He also has a place in musical history as founder-conductor of the world-famous Vienna Philharmonic Orchestra.

Nielsen, Carl (1865–1931).
Danish composer, generally regarded as his country's greatest. Like his exact contemporary Sibelius in Finland, Nielsen reacted against the weighty, emotional character of late Romantic and post-Wagnerian music with a series of symphonies which are, by comparison, fresh and direct in content and form. Of his six symphonies, no 2 is called 'The Four Temperaments' (its movements being based on the old idea of the four aspects of human personality— choleric, phlegmatic, melancholic, sanguine), no 3 is *Sinfonia Espansiva*, and no 4 is the 'Unquenchable' (sometimes translated as 'Inextinguishable'). He also wrote operas, orchestral concertos for various instruments, concert overtures, and chamber music.

Obrecht, Jacob (about 1451–1505).
Netherlands composer, noted for his use of melodies from secular *chansons* and folk songs in his church masses and motets, and for the comparatively warm and spontaneous character of much of his music.

Ockeghem, Jean de
(about 1425–95).
Netherlands composer, in service to the French court for many years. He was also a great and influential teacher, known among his contemporaries as 'The Prince of Music'. Ockeghem's elaborate polyphonic style, in which the individual melodic lines, or parts, often follow one another in an 'imitative' way, helped to prepare the way for the fugues and similar contrapuntal works of Bach, over two hundred years later. He also wrote secular French *chansons*.

Jacques Offenbach

Ignacy Paderewski

Offenbach, Jacques (1819–80).
German born but by adoption a French composer, achieving tremendous success with a series of nearly ninety tuneful and light-hearted operettas. The best known of these today are *La Belle Hélène* and *Orpheus in the Underworld* (containing the famous can-can). His opera *The Tales of Hoffmann* (based on the work of the German writer E.T.A. Hoffmann) is more serious in character.

Oliver, Joseph 'King' (1885–1938).
American cornet player and band leader, and one of the pioneers of jazz. He led a band in the Storeyville district of New Orleans between 1910 and 1917, then moved to Chicago, forming his famous Creole Jazz Band and making some of the finest recordings in the best New Orleans style. Louis Armstrong worked closely with him for some years.

Orff, Carl (born 1895).
German composer and prominent figure in the field of musical education. He composed operas and other stage works; but his best-known work today is the *Carmina Burana*, a type of cantata, setting to music medieval verses mostly to do with drinking and love, and written in a bright and entertaining style.

Ory, Edward 'Kid' (1889–1973).
American jazz trombonist and band leader, working with Joe 'King' Oliver, 'Jelly Roll' Morton, Louis Armstrong, Sidney Bechet and other leading exponents of early jazz. He continued playing, on and off, right up to the 1960s, his composition 'Muskrat Ramble' having become a big hit.

Paderewski, Ignacy (1860–1941).
Polish pianist of immense popularity during the earlier part of this century, also composer. He became the first Prime Minister of the newly founded Polish state in 1919 and later Speaker of the exiled Polish parliament at the outbreak of the Second World War.

Above: Giovanni Pierluigi da Palestrina

Right: Adelina Patti

Paganini, Niccolò (1782–1840).
Italian violinist, and the most celebrated of all virtuoso violin players on account of his almost freakish command of the instrument. This, and his awkward, cadaverous appearance, gave rise to legends associating him with the Devil—which all helped to draw the crowds wherever he went. As a composer Paganini wrote five violin concertos and a number of works for solo violin which reflect his astonishing technique. One of his capriccios is very well known because Brahms, Rachmaninov and others have used it as the basis for compositions of their own.

Palestrina, Giovanni Pierluigi da (about 1525–94).
Italian composer (named after his birthplace near Rome). He spent most of his life in service to the Pope, creating a 'pure' polyphonic style in his masses, motets and other religious works that has been highly regarded since. His *Missa Papae Marcelli* ('Mass for Pope Marcellus') was long believed to have saved music from being banned in church at the time of the Roman Catholic Counter-Reformation, on account of its heaven-inspired beauty, but there is probably no historical truth in this. Palestrina also composed some madrigals, and outside church affairs he was a successful businessman.

Parker, Charlie 'Bird' (1920–55).
American jazz saxophonist and one of the most original and daring of jazz musicians. With trumpeter Dizzy Gillespie, pianist Thelonius Monk and a few others, he created the style known as Bebop, which broke up all existing jazz conventions and opened the way for even more radical styles. Like some of the other most gifted jazz musicians, Parker could not stand up to the pressures of his way of life and died young from drink and drugs.

Patti, Adelina (1843–1919).
Italian operatic soprano whose parents settled in the United States when she was a child. She achieved fame and fortune, notably for her singing of the *bel canto* roles in Bellini, Donizetti and Rossini, and for her parts in French opera.

Pedrell, Felipe (1841–1922).
Spanish musical historian who edited and revived much old Spanish music. He is also regarded as founder of the Spanish nationalist school, being the teacher of Granados and Falla.

Pergolesi, Giovanni Battista (1710–36).
Italian composer, mainly of operas, whose *La Serva padrona* ('The Maid as Mistress') in the *opera buffa* style caused a big quarrel between the supporters of Italian and French opera—known as the 'War of the Buffoons'—when it was staged in Paris. Stravinsky's ballet *Pulcinella* is loosely based on Pergolesi's music.

Peri, Jacopo (1561–1633).
Italian priest and composer, and member of the group of musicians and other artists known as the *Camerata* ('Fellowship'), whose attempted revival of Classical Greek drama is regarded as the true beginning of opera. In this context, Peri's *Euridice* was one of the first operas to be staged.

Pérotin, or Perotinus Magnus (about 1160–1220).
French choirmaster and composer, and, with his older colleague Léonin, associated with the so-called Notre Dame School of music in Paris. They were both pioneers in early forms of polyphony, their work belonging to what is known as the *ars antiqua*, or Old Art, as distinct from the *ars nova*, or New Art, of their successors.

Porter, Cole (1893–1964).
American song-writer who composed the lyrics—often extremely witty and sophisticated—as well as the melodies to most of his songs. Among his celebrated numbers are 'Let's Do It', 'You're the Top' and 'Night and Day'; his many successful stage and film musicals include *Kiss Me Kate* (based on Shakespeare's *The Taming of the Shrew*), *Can Can* and *High Society*. He was crippled by a riding accident and lived in constant pain for many years after.

Poulenc, Francis (1899–1963).
French pianist and composer, and originally a member of the group called 'Les Six'. He developed a clear and elegant style, but one capable of expressing real feeling. His works include the opera *Les Dialogues des Carmélites* (a story of Carmelite nuns during the French Revolution), the ballet *Les Biches*, several concertos, piano pieces, and many songs.

Praetorius
The Latin name taken by many sixteenth- and seventeenth-century German musicians. Most famous is Michael Praetorius (1571–1621), who composed motets, madrigals and instrumental pieces, and also wrote a book which sums up the musical knowledge and thinking of his time.

Prokofiev, Sergei (1891–1953).
Soviet Russian pianist and composer. He left the Soviet Union soon after the Bolshevik Revolution, composing music noted at the time for its difficulty and dissonance. Returning to his homeland, he modified his style in accordance with Soviet policy, producing music with a much wider appeal. His works include seven symphonies—no 1 is the popular 'Classical' Symphony; several concertos; piano sonatas and other instrumental works; the opera *War and Peace* (based on Tolstoy's novel); the ballets *Cinderella* and *Romeo and Juliet* (after Shakespeare); *Peter and the Wolf* (a Russian folk tale for narrator and orchestra); and music for several films, notably *Lieutenant Kije* and some which were directed by Sergei Eisenstein.

Sergei Prokofiev

Puccini in yachting gear, with his young niece.

Henry Purcell

Puccini, Giacomo (1858–1924). Italian composer, almost exclusively of opera. His output was small compared with that of his great predecessor Verdi, but five of the operas he did produce are now among the most popular in the repertory, combining beautifully constructed melodies with a clear and vivid orchestration. They are *Manon Lescaut*, *La Bohème*, *Tosca*, *Madame Butterfly* and *Turandot* (completed by Franco Alfano after his death). His one-act comedy *Gianni Schicchi* (forming part of a group of three one-act operas called *Il Trittico*, or 'The Triptych') is also a great favourite. Another interesting opera is *La Fanciulla del West* ('The Girl of the Golden West'), set in California at the time of the famous gold-rush. Puccini also contributed to the operatic style called *verismo* ('realism'), with its emphasis on basic human emotions or situations.

Purcell, Henry (1659–95). English composer, remembered today especially for his stage works, including the opera *Dido and Aeneas* which has some of the most expressive music ever set to English words; and *The Fairy Queen*, a semi-operatic version of Shakespeare's *A Midsummer Night's Dream*. Purcell also wrote several cantata-like pieces called odes, intended for special occasions, and instrumental compositions, including the so-called 'Golden' Sonata. The well-known 'Trumpet Voluntary', long attributed to him, is now known to be by his close contemporary Jeremiah Clarke and was originally called 'The Prince of Denmark's March'.

Quantz, Johann Joachim (1697–1773) German composer, mainly of music for the flute. He was employed by Frederick the Great, teaching his royal master to play the instrument.

Quilter, Roger (1877–1953) English composer of many attractive songs and *A Children's Overture*.

Sergei Rachmaninov

Rachmaninov, Sergei Vassilievich (1873–1943).

Russian pianist and composer. He left Russia soon after the Bolshevik Revolution, finally settling in the United States; but he remained deeply attached in a spiritual sense to his homeland, expressing his feelings in music written in a late Romantic style and characteristically melancholy mood. His principal compositions are: four piano concertos, plus the Rhapsody on a Theme of Paganini; three symphonies; the symphonic poem *The Isle of the Dead* (inspired by a painting of the same name); a cantata *The Bells* (after the poem by Edgar Allen Poe); Symphonic Dances for orchestra; and many pieces for solo piano. As a pianist—possibly the greatest of his generation—Rachmaninov made recordings of his own and other composers' music.

Rameau, Jean Philippe (1683–1764).

French organist, harpsichordist and composer. For many years he concentrated, like his older colleague Couperin, on the composition of keyboard music, then produced a series of spectacular and very strikingly written opera-ballets, including *Les Indes Galantes* ('The Courtly Indies'). It was his operas and those of the Italian Pergolesi that produced the musical controversy called 'The War of the Buffoons'. Rameau also wrote several important books on musical theory, which are now interesting for the light they throw on eighteenth-century musical thinking.

Ravel, Maurice (1875–1937).

French composer and colleague of Fauré, Debussy, Satie and members of 'Les Six'. His music expresses something of the character of each of these people or groups in turn, while developing along very individual lines of its own. Ravel was a superb orchestrator, his masterpiece in this field being his score to the ballet *Daphnis et Chloé*. Other great examples of his orchestration can be heard in the operas *L'Enfant et les sortilèges* (loosely translated as 'The Spellbound Child', with libretto by Colette) and *L'Heure Espagnole* ('The Spanish Hour'); the orchestral song-cycle *Shéhérazade*; the two jazz-influenced piano concertos (one for the left hand only) and the *Bolero*. His piano music includes the impressionistic *Miroirs* ('Mirrors', including 'Alborada del gracioso'), *Mother Goose* suite and *Gaspard de la Nuit* ('Phantoms of the Night'); also pieces modelled on past styles, *Valses Nobles et Sentimentales* and *Le Tombeau de Couperin* (much of this music being later orchestrated by the composer). Ravel also wrote several notable chamber music and instrumental works—a string quartet, piano trio, Introduction and Allegro for clarinet flute, harp and string quartet, and a violin sonata.

Maurice Ravel

Reinhardt, Django (1910–53). Belgian gipsy guitarist, and the first great European jazz musician. His left hand was severely burned in a caravan fire, which forced him to give up the violin in favour of the guitar, but he teamed up with the violinist Stephane Grappelly, to lead the unique Quintet of the Hot Club de France. This famous group broke up at the start of the Second World War, but Reinhardt continued playing, and just after the war made some appearances with Duke Ellington.

Respighi, Ottorino (1879-1936). Italian composer of two dazzling orchestral pieces, *The Pines of Rome* and *The Fountains of Rome*, but also of more restrained works such as *Three Botticelli Pictures* and the orchestral suite *The Birds* (based on music of the seventeenth and eighteenth centuries, and reflecting Respighi's scholarly interest in old music). Another of his works is the ballet *La Boutique fantasque* ('The Fantastic Toyshop'), based on music by Rossini.

Riegger, Wallingford (1885–1961). American composer. He studied in Germany for some years, developing a style based partly on twelve-tone methods of composition. His works include three symphonies, and much music for the Martha Graham and other dance companies.

Rimsky-Korsakov, Nicolai Andreivich (1844–1908). Russian composer, and leading member of the nationalist group known as 'The Five'. He started life as a naval officer, and only began to develop his own style of composition after he had been appointed as a professor to the St Petersburg Musical Conservatory. Above all, Rimsky-Korsakov was a gifted and inspired orchestrator, his works including the operas *The Snow Maiden* and *The Golden Cockerel* (a work of political satire that was banned in Russia until after his death), the

Nicolai Rimsky-Korsakov

orchestral suite *Sheherazade* (inspired by *Tales from the Arabian Nights*), the *Capriccio Espagnol* ('Spanish Caprice') and the *Russian Easter Festival* overture. He also undertook completion or revision of the work of several of his colleagues, notably of Mussorgsky's *Boris Godunov* and Borodin's *Prince Igor*.

Rossini, Gioacchino (1792–1868). Italian composer of operas, serious and comic, in the *bel canto* style of his time. A particularly striking feature of his music consists of the gradual building-up of a small but significant phrase into a splendid climax, a custom which earned him the title of 'Signor Crescendo'. His operas include *La Scala di seta* ('The Silken Ladder'), *La Gazza ladra* ('The Thieving Magpie'), *La Cenerentola* ('Cinderella'), *Semiramide*, *The Barber*

of Seville (which has some of the same characters as Mozart's 'The Marriage of Figaro', but not the same plot), and *William Tell* (based on Friedrich Schiller's play about the legendary Swiss hero). This opera, written for the Paris stage, was also his last. From the time of its successful production until his death nearly forty years later, Rossini lived in semi-retirement in Paris. The few further works he did produce, such as the songs and duets published as *Soirées Musicales* ('Musical Evenings'), he humorously called 'sins of my old age'.

Ruggles, Carl (1876–1971). American composer who created a strongly individual style in such works as the symphonic poems *Men and Mountains* and *Sun-Treader*, and *Angels* for six trumpets. He was also a painter.

Camille Saint-Saëns

Saint-Saëns, Camille (1835–1921). French organist, pianist and composer. He composed in a generally clear and melodious style, and in practically every existing musical form. Many of his largest works— his operas and three symphonies (no 3 with organ)—are not regularly performed today; but others remain favourite concert pieces such as the *Danse Macabre*; and the humorous *Le Carnaval des animaux* ('The Carnival of the Animals', subtitled 'grand zoological fantasy') for two pianos and orchestra, which includes the piece called 'The Swan'.

Sarasate, Pablo de (1844–1908). Spanish violinist and one of the greatest virtuoso players of his time. He also composed a number of violin works and had others written specially for him, notably the 'Spanish' Symphony (really a concerto) by the French composer Edouard Lalo.

Satie, Erik (1866–1925). French composer, though his mother was Scottish. He composed mainly for the piano, producing, in works like the three pieces called *Gymnopédie*, music of typically French elegance and refinement. Other pieces, with such startling titles as *Trois Morceaux en forme de poire* ('Three Pear-shaped Pieces') and *Embryons desséchés* ('Dried-up Embryos'), represent his strong reaction against the heavy, emotional character of late Romantic music; and in this respect he had considerable influence on the group of young French composers known as 'Les Six'. He did, however, write one quite 'serious' work, a type of cantata called *Socrate,* based on Plato's writings.

Scarlatti, Alessandro (1660–1725). Italian composer of many masses, cantatas, madrigals, also much instrumental music, but now chiefly remembered for his operas, whose style influenced Handel and many other eighteenth-century operatic composers. His son **Domenico** (1685–1757) also wrote some operas, but his most important works are reckoned to be his keyboard sonatas (over 500 in number), which made a big contribution to the development of Classical sonata form. Many of these sonatas (or 'exercises' as they were often called in Domenico Scarlatti's own lifetime) are delightful pieces in their own right; one of them is nicknamed 'Cat's Fugue'.

Schnabel, Artur (1882–1951). Austrian pianist who settled in the United States after the Nazis came to power. His playing marked an end to the grand Romantic style and the start of a much more controlled style of performance. Beethoven was his speciality.

Schoenberg, Arnold (1874–1951). Austrian composer who worked first in Germany then, after the Nazi rise to power, in the United States. His early compositions, such as *Verklärte Nacht* ('Transfigured Night') and *Gurrelieder* ('Songs of Gurra', for solo singers, chorus and orchestra) are written in a heavily late Romantic, post-Wagnerian style. It was Schoenberg's reaction against this style, and his creation of an entirely new method of composition, called twelve-tone, dodecaphonic or serial composition, that made him one of the most influential figures in twentieth-century music. Works moving towards this new style, or employing it to a greater or lesser extent, include *Erwartung* ('Expectation'), which is like a short opera for one character; the cantata *A Survivor from Warsaw* (about Nazi crimes against Jews); the unfinished opera *Moses and Aaron*; also some orchestral, instrumental and piano pieces. Schoenberg's originality and influence went further with his song-cycle called *Pierrot Lunaire* ('Moonstruck Pierrot'), in which he first used in a fully developed form a performing style called *Sprechgesang* ('speech-song'). In this, as the term suggests, the singer hovers half-way between speaking and singing.

Schubert, Franz (1797–1828). Austrian composer who lived and died in Vienna and received almost no recognition during his own short lifetime. Some of his music was only rediscovered years after his death. Schubert continued the so-called Viennese tradition of Haydn, Mozart and Beethoven; he composed nine symphonies—no 4 in C minor is called 'Tragic', no 8 in B minor is the so-called 'Unfinished' because it has only two movements, no 9 in C major is called 'the Great C major'— also a string quintet, string quartets and piano sonatas in a basically Classical form; plus many short piano pieces such as the Impromptus and the group called *Moments Musicaux* ('Musical Moments'). But it is as a composer of *Lieder* (songs) that he is generally regarded as the first great figure of Romantic music. Schubert wrote over six hundred songs—all to existing poems—some rarely performed, others among the best-loved pieces in all music. Famous individual *Lieder* are: 'Heidenröslein' ('Wayside Rose'), 'Gretchen am Spinnrade' ('Gretchen at the Spinning-Wheel'), 'Der Erlkönig, ('The Erl King') and 'An die Musik' ('To Music'). Greatest are the song-cycles *Die schöne Müllerin* ('The Fair Maid of the Mill') and *Die Winterreise* ('The Winter Journey'); also the group of *Lieder* published posthumously under the title *Schwanengesang* ('Swan Song'). Schubert used some of his *Lieder* again in instrumental compositions, notably in the 'Trout' Quintet and in the String Quartet in D minor, 'Death and the Maiden'. There are also the overture and incidental music

to the play *Rosamunde*, though the overture that now goes under that title was originally intended for a different stage work. Schubert's works have been catalogued by the scholar Otto Deutsch and are often quoted with their 'Deutsch' or 'D' number.

Schuman, William (born 1910). American composer, many of whose works are inspired by some aspect of native American music, including jazz. Among these are *A William Billings Overture* and *New England Triptych* (both using themes by the early American composer William Billings) and the *American Festival Overture*. Other compositions include eight symphonies, a piano and a violin concerto and the opera *The Mighty Casey*, which has baseball as its theme.

Franz Schubert as a very young man.

Robert Schumann

Schumann, Robert (1810–56). German composer of some of the finest Romantic music, especially for the piano—*Papillons* ('Butterflies'), *Carnaval* (based on the notes which correspond, in German, to the letters of a place name connected with the composer's private life), *Kreisleriana* (inspired by a character from the stories of E.T.A. Hoffmann), *Kinderscenen* ('Scenes of Childhood') and *Davidsbündler-Tänze* ('Dances of the League of David', inspired by Schumann's imaginary 'League of David', or group of progressive young musicians). He was also a great *Lieder* composer with his song-cycles *Dichterliebe* ('Poet's Love') and *Frauenliebe und -leben* ('Woman's Love and Life'). Other compositions include four symphonies—no 1 is the 'Spring', no 3 the 'Rhenish'—the very popular Piano Concerto in A minor, and chamber music. In addition, Schumann was a noted musical journalist and critic. His wife Clara (her maiden name was Wieck) was a brilliant pianist and composer in her own right. After Robert's tragic mental breakdown and death, she became one of Brahms's closest friends and musical colleagues.

Schütz, Heinrich (1585–1672). German composer who studied for some years with Giovanni Gabrieli in Venice, and was an important link between Italian music of the Renaissance and German music of the Baroque period. In particular, his settings of the Passion served as a model for Bach when he came to write his St John and St Matthew Passions.

Scriabin, Alexander (1872–1915). Russian pianist and composer who progressed from a Romantic, Chopin-like style of composition in his sonatas and other piano pieces to music of harmonic originality and daring. This was prompted by his deep interest in Theosophy, a kind of occult religion with a world-wide following during his lifetime.

Andrés Segovia

Scriabin devised what he called a 'mystic chord'—really a new kind of scale—using this in several orchestral works, including *Prometheus, the Poem of Fire*. He also invented a 'keyboard of colour' which related colours to notes and was intended to project these onto a screen; but it was never used.

Segovia, Andrés (born 1893). Spanish guitarist who has done more than anyone else to establish the guitar as a serious concert instrument.

His playing has inspired compositions from his fellow countryman Manuel de Falla and others.

Shaw, Artie (born 1910). American jazz clarinettist and band leader, and one of the biggest names during the swing era of the 1930s and 1940s. He recorded several times with Blues singer Billie Holiday, and made some of his most successful discs with an ensemble called The Gramercy Five, including 'Special Delivery Stomp' and 'Summit Ridge Drive'.

101

Shostakovich, Dmitri (1906–75). Soviet Russian composer, now honoured in his own country as one of the greatest Soviet artists, although there were times when his work was severely criticized by the authorities because it was considered too difficult and advanced, or not sufficiently patriotic in spirit. In fact, Shostakovich's career was constantly marked by his efforts to reconcile his own creative style with his duty as a Soviet artist to serve the needs of state and people. His largest body of music is contained in his fifteen symphonies, some of which carry a strong political or patriotic theme—no 7, the 'Leningrad' Symphony, was partly composed in that city during its terrible period of siege in the Second World War. Other works include concertos for various instruments, an important group of string quartets, and much piano music; also the opera originally called *Lady Macbeth of Mtsensk District* (soon after renamed *Katerina Ismailova*) which was one of the works that got him into political trouble.

Sibelius, Jean (1865–1957). Finnish composer, and his country's greatest musical figure. His most important works are his seven symphonies, which as a group show his progress towards a very distinctive orchestral style, noted for its economical, sometimes quite sparse scoring and concentration of ideas (the Seventh Symphony being condensed into one continuous and relatively short movement). From another point of view, these symphonies represent Sibelius's reaction against the heavy and complex orchestral style of post-Wagnerian composers like Mahler and Richard Strauss. Many people also consider them, and the Violin Concerto in D minor, to represent much of the character of his native land. Sibelius wrote other orchestral works which are more openly programmatic, such as the tone poems *En Saga*, *The Swan of*

Dmitri Shostakovich

Jean Sibelius

Tuonela and *Tapiola*, inspired by either the spirit or the imagery of Finnish myth and legend; also the early *Finlandia* which has become a kind of patriotic hymn. Another popular composition is the *Valse Triste*. Sibelius, like Rossini, suddenly stopped composing, producing virtually nothing more during the last thirty years of his life.

Skalkottas, Nikos (1904–49). Greek violinist and composer, a pupil and musical follower of Schoenberg, but also a nationalist composer in the way he made use of Greek folk songs and dances. He received very little recognition in his own lifetime, most of his compositions—the Greek Dances for orchestra, piano concertos and instrumental works—being published only after his death.

Smetana, Bedřich (1824–84). Bohemian-Czech pianist, conductor and composer, and founder of the Czech national style or school of music. As a conductor, he helped to establish a Czech national opera in Prague and became its leading musical figure. As a composer he made great use of Czech folk song

and dance, in his opera *The Bartered Bride*, and in his largest orchestral work *Ma Vlast* ('My Country' or 'My Fatherland'), which is a group of tone poems depicting different aspects of the Czech landscape or history. Like Beethoven, Smetana went deaf, alluding to this affliction in his String Quartet in E minor, called *From my Life*, by the use of a very high, bleak-sounding violin note.

Smith, Bessie (about 1896–1938). Jazz vocalist, who started her career with hot gospel and Blues singer Ma Rainey and became the most famous interpreter of the Blues. Her greatest period was during the 1920s, after which her style began to go out of fashion and personal problems affected her performance. Tragically, she died after a car accident.

Solti, Sir Georg (born 1912). Hungarian-born conductor, Musical Director of the Covent Garden Opera for ten years, also closely associated with several orchestras, including the Chicago Symphony Orchestra, and noted for the dynamic character of his performances. He is also a pianist.

Kandy dancers from Sri Lanka.

A guitarist from the Fiji Islands.

A calypso band in Jamaica.

John Philip Sousa

Karlheinz Stockhausen

Sousa, John Philip (1854–1932). American military band leader and composer. He raised playing standards in his own bands to a high professional level, and lived up to his own claim that 'a march should make a man with a wooden leg want to step out' by composing some of the very finest marches, including 'The Washington Post' and 'The Stars and Stripes Forever'. The sousaphone, a large brass wind instrument designed to encircle the player's body, is named after him.

Spohr, Ludwig (1784–1859). German violinist, conductor and composer. He produced a very large quantity of music—operas and oratorios, symphonies and concertos, and much chamber music—in a tuneful, Romantic style that made him for a long time one of the most popular of composers. He was a pioneer figure in the modern art of conducting, being among the first to use a baton.

Stamitz, Johann Wenzel (1717–57). Bohemian-born violinist and composer (the original version of his name being Stamič). He was Musical Director at the Court of Mannheim and founder of the so-called Mannheim School of musicians who contributed much to the development of the symphony, concerto, sonata and other eighteenth-century Classical forms. Johann and his son **Karl** (1745–1801) both composed symphonies and other works in the new Classical style of their time.

Still, William Grant (born 1895). American composer and the first black American to compose and conduct a large symphonic work— the 'Afro-American' Symphony. His other works include the opera *Troubled Island* (about Haiti), and *Lenox Avenue* for chorus and orchestra (portraying Harlem, the black quarter of New York).

Stockhausen, Karlheinz (born 1928). German composer and one of the most imaginative and inventive figures of late twentieth-century music. He has based some of his compositions on the twelve-tone methods of Schoenberg and Webern, made extensive use of electronic apparatus, and developed the possibilities of indeterminacy, which leaves certain options open to performers. His works include *Gruppen* for three orchestral groups, *Zyklus* for percussion player, *Kontakte* for electronic sounds, piano and percussion, *Hymnen* (being an electronic treatment of various national anthems), and *Stimmung* ('Tuning' or 'Atmosphere') for six voices electronically controlled. The first composer to publish a fully electronic score in the form of diagrams, Stockhausen is also a lively teacher and lecturer, especially on behalf of his own ideas and music.

Johann Strauss the Younger

Richard Strauss

Strauss, Johann, the elder

(1804–1849) and **the younger** (1825–1899). Austrian violinists, conductors and composers. As father and son they built up the waltz into the most popular dance of all time, and were enormously successful in the process. In fact, Johann Strauss the elder is best remembered today for his *Radetzky March* (named after an Austrian general), while it was his son who wrote such famous waltzes as 'The Blue Danube' and 'Tales from the Vienna Woods'. Johann Strauss the younger was equally successful in the field of operetta, his masterpiece here being *Die Fledermaus* ('The Bat'). His brothers Eduard and Josef were also composers of waltzes and other dances such as the polka.

Strauss, Richard (1864–1949).

German composer, generally regarded as the last great figure in the tradition of German Romantic music. His early compositions were a series of symphonic poems, written for a very large post-Wagnerian orchestra, which amazed the musical world of the time with their vivid and sometimes startling descriptive effects. These include *Don Juan*, *Till Eulenspiegel* (episodes in the life of a German folk hero), *Also Sprach Zarathustra* ('Thus Spake Zarathustra', inspired by the writings of the philosopher Nietzsche), *Don Quixote* (based on the famous novel by Cervantes), and *Ein Heldenleben* ('A Hero's Life', really an autobiographical study in music). Strauss then turned his attention to opera. *Salome* (based on Oscar Wilde's play, not the Bible) and *Elektra* (from the play by Sophocles) shocked early audiences with their lurid scenes and accompanying music. *Der Rosenkavalier* ('The Cavalier of the Rose', a love story set in eighteenth-century Vienna) marked the high point of his collaboration with the librettist Hugo von Hofmannsthal, and was his greatest success. *Ariadne auf Naxos* and other operas followed. He also wrote many *Lieder* (songs), some with orchestral accompaniment, and two of the finest concertos for the horn. Strauss remained, rather unhappily, in Germany after the Nazis came to power, and was ruined by the Second World War.

Igor Stravinsky as a young man

Sir Arthur Sullivan

Stravinsky, Igor (1882–1971). Russian-born composer who lived in France for many years before finally settling in the United States and becoming an American citizen. He rose swiftly to fame in the years just before the First World War with the three progressively more brilliant and adventurous scores he produced for the Diaghilev Ballet—*The Firebird* (based on a Russian fairy tale), *Petrushka* (portraying the tragic existence of the traditional Russian puppet Petrushka, or 'Little Pete'), and *The Rite of Spring* (produced in France with the title *Le Sacre du printemps*, and portraying pagan rites in ancient Russia). The war put an end to such big productions, and Stravinsky started to compose on a much smaller scale—*The Soldier's Tale* (for three actors and a small jazz-style band), *Les Noces* ('The Wedding', for chorus and soloists, four pianos and percussion). He also entered his so-called 'Neo-Classical' period, composing such works as the Octet for Wind Instruments and the opera-oratorio *Oedipus Rex* (based on a play by Sophocles) in a very cool, unemotional style. The Symphony of Psalms, Symphony in Three Movements, the opera *The Rake's Progress* (inspired by Hogarth's series of paintings of the same name) and other works mark his gradual return to a more expressive style; and in his final group of works, including further ballet scores, he made use of twelve-tone methods of composition. Like his almost exact contemporary, the artist Pablo Picasso, Stravinsky's creative life passed through a number of distinct periods or styles, and he remained one of music's most influential figures during the first half of this century and beyond.

Sullivan, Sir Arthur (1842–1900). English organist, conductor and composer who helped to re-establish the name of English music and musicians after a long period of decline, with his symphony, cantata *The Golden Legend* and several other 'serious' works. It was, however, his long partnership with the librettist W.S. Gilbert that has won him lasting fame. Their tremendously successful series of comic operettas include *Trial by Jury*, *HMS Pinafore*, *The Pirates of Penzance*, *Patience*, *Iolanthe*, *Ruddigore*, *The Mikado*, *The Yeomen of the Guard* and *The Gondoliers*. Music from them has been used in the ballet *Pineapple Poll* which is based on a story by Gilbert.

Suppé, Franz von (1819–95). Austrian composer of many once-popular operettas, the overture to *Light Cavalry* still being a popular concert piece. Another is the overture he wrote to the play *Poet and Peasant*.

Sutherland, Joan (born 1926). Australian operatic soprano who has gained a world-wide reputation for her singing of the great *bel canto* roles, mainly in the operas of Bellini and Donizetti.

Sweelinck, Jan Pieterszoon
(1562–1621).
Dutch organist and composer. He
greatly advanced organ technique in
his compositions, especially in the
writing of fugues for the instrument,
and had a big influence on the
development of organ music in
Holland and Germany up to the time
of Bach. Like Schütz, he studied in
Venice for a time, and this inspired
him to write some fine choral music
also.

Tallis, Thomas (about 1505–85).
English organist and composer. With
his younger colleague William Byrd,
Tallis lived through the very
disturbed religious period of English
history that involved the break with
the authority of the Pope and
eventual establishment of the
Anglican Church. Despite these
troubles, he composed religious
music, to texts both in Latin and in
English, of great solemnity and polyphonic skill. His Latin motet *Spem in
alium* is, in fact, one of the high
points in the whole history of polyphonic music, being written for eight
small choirs of five voices each, and
having forty separate parts. As one of
the most eminent musicians of his
time, Tallis shared with Byrd the sole
right to print music in England.

Tartini, Giuseppe (1692–1770).
Italian violinist and composer. He
was a great innovator in the field of
violin construction and playing technique, especially with regard to the
design and use of new kinds of bow.
He also wrote some important books
on musical theory and the physics of
acoustics. As a composer, Tartini is
best remembered for his so-called
'Devil's Trill' Sonata, said to have
been inspired by a dream in which
the Devil appeared before him
playing the violin.

Tatum, Arthur or 'Art' (1910–56).
American jazz pianist. He raised jazz
playing standards to a virtuoso level
which amazed such fellow pianists as

Peter Ilich Tchaikovsky

Walter Gieseking and Vladimir
Horowitz when they first heard him.
He had, at the same time, a subtle and
often complex rhythmic sense and a
feeling for harmonies sometimes
reminiscent of Debussy. Almost
blind since childhood, Art Tatum
maintained the same brilliant
standards from the late 1920s right up
to the year of his death, and his
influence on other jazz pianists, such
as the Canadian Oscar Peterson, has
been immense.

Taverner, John (about 1495–1545).
English composer who was
appointed by Cardinal Wolsey to the
post of organist and choirmaster at
what is now Christ Church
Cathedral, Oxford, and produced
some of the finest English Latin
church music, including eight
settings of the Mass. Later in life his
conversion to Protestantism and his
part in the break-up of the English
monasteries diverted him from
music.

Tchaikovsky, Peter Ilich
(1840–93).
The first Russian composer to become internationally famous and one
of the most popular of all the great
composers. His success took him on
concert tours of Europe and the
United States, but he remained a
basically unhappy man, disturbed by
personal problems. His long association (virtually all by correspondence)
with his private patron Madame
Nadezhda von Meck was a big source
of encouragement as well as financial
security, and it was a great blow to
his feelings when she broke it off. He
died after drinking untreated water
during an outbreak of cholera in St
Petersburg. Tchaikovsky's music,
though typically Russian in some
respects, is less consciously so than
that of his nationalist colleagues
known as 'The Five'. He composed
mostly in established musical forms,
like the symphony and concerto,
adding to them his own special gifts
for dramatic orchestration and grand
melody, together with a fair degree
of personal expression—all in the late
Romantic manner of his day. His
principal works are: six
symphonies—no 1 ('Winter
Daydreams'), no 2 ('Little Russian'),
no 3 ('Polish'), no 6 ('Pathétique');
also the 'Manfred' Symphony (based
on the subject of a poem by Byron);
three piano concertos (no 1 in B flat
minor being the famous one); a violin
concerto; the symphonic poems (or
fantasy-overtures) *Romeo and Juliet*,
Hamlet and *Francesca da Rimini* (based
on the poetry of Dante); the operas
Eugene Onegin and *The Queen of
Spades*; the three celebrated ballet
scores to *Swan Lake*, *The Sleeping
Beauty* and *The Nutcracker*; and the
overture *1812*.

Telemann, Georg Philipp
(1681–1767).
German composer whose output—
very large even by the prolific
standards of his time—includes about
forty operas, forty oratorios, six
hundred orchestral works and many

Sir Michael Tippett

more instrumental and vocal pieces.
His music is of interest because it
marks the transition from the early
eighteenth-century Baroque style of
Bach and Handel to the later
eighteenth-century Rococo and
Classical styles of Haydn and Mozart.
A very successful man, he was for
some years director of music in the
City of Hamburg.

Thomson, Virgil (born 1896).
American composer who studied in
Europe, but has made frequent use of
traditional American music, such as
the old revivalist hymn tunes, in his
own works. These include the operas
Four Saints in Three Acts and *The
Mother of Us All* (both with librettos
by the famous writer Gertrude
Stein). He has also been an eminent
music critic.

Tippett, Sir Michael Kemp
(born 1905).
English composer who, like his compatriots Vaughan Williams and
Benjamin Britten, has sometimes
linked his own music to great English
music of past times. He has also made
use of Negro spirituals and jazz. His
works include the operas *The
Midsummer Marriage*, *King Priam* and
The Knot Garden, the oratorio *A
Child of our Time*, symphonies, string
quartets and other instrumental compositions, and song-cycles.

Torelli, Giuseppe (1658–1709).
Italian violinist and composer who,
with his fellow countryman Corelli,
was one of the pioneer figures in the
development of the concerto grosso
and other new musical forms for the
violin family of instruments.

Arturo Toscanini

Vaughan Williams, Ralph
(1872–1958).
English composer whose main sources of inspiration were English folk music and English music of past times, giving much of his own music a distinctive, nationalistic sound. His compositions include nine symphonies—no 1 ('Sea'), no 2 ('London'), no 3 ('Pastoral') and no 7 (*Sinfonia Antartica*, taken from his score to the film *Scott of the Antarctic*); Fantasia on a Theme of Thomas Tallis; overture to Aristophanes' play *The Wasps*; the opera *Pilgrim's Progress* (after the novel by John Bunyan); the ballet *Job* (inspired by William Blake's illustrations to the Book of Job); *The Lark Ascending* for violin and orchestra; the song-cycle *On Wenlock Edge* (to poems by A.E. Housman); and many folk song arrangements, notably the Fantasia on 'Greensleeves'.

Verdi, Giuseppe (1813–1901).
Italian operatic composer. He was born in the northern Italian district of Parma, and the background to most of his career was the long campaign leading to a politically united Italy. When he died, in Milan, he was beloved as a person and revered, through his music, as one of the greatest heroes of his country. He progressed slowly but surely as a composer, his work constantly gaining in assurance and dramatic force, until he had created a style of continuous musical and dramatic development quite similar in some respects to Wagner's music-drama. His most famous operas are: *Rigoletto* (based on a play by Victor Hugo), *La Traviata* (which can be translated as 'The Woman Gone Astray', and is based on a novel and play by Alexandre Dumas the younger), *Il Trovatore* ('The Troubadour'), *Simon Boccanegra*, *Un Ballo in Maschera* ('A Masked Ball'), *La Forza del Destino* ('The Force of Destiny'), *Don Carlos*, *Aida* (intended to celebrate the opening of the Suez Canal), *Otello* and *Falstaff* (these last two

Toscanini, Arturo (1867–1957).
Italian conductor, renowned for his attention to detail and for the drive and power of his performances. He was also one of the first to conduct regularly without a score, a habit prompted in his case by extreme short-sightedness. He was already a world-famous figure when the National Broadcasting Company (NBC) Symphony Orchestra was specially created for him in New York, and he made some of his most celebrated recordings with them. Included among them are his dynamic interpretations of the Beethoven symphonies.

Varèse, Edgar (1885–1965).
French-born composer who lived and worked mainly in the United States. He was a very advanced musical thinker, exploring many new sound possibilities, including the use of electronic instruments, ahead of most of his colleagues. He also gave some of his compositions unusual scientific sounding titles, such as *Density 21.5* (a piece for solo flute) and *Ionization* (for percussion instruments). Varèse expressed his own attitude to his work as a so-called *avant-garde* composer by saying 'an artist is never ahead of his time. Most people are behind theirs!'

Ralph Vaughan Williams—portrait by Sir Gerald Kelly

Shakespearian adaptations being the fruit of Verdi's collaboration with Arrigo Boito as librettist). Verdi also composed a famous setting of the Requiem Mass, prompted by the death of his friend, the writer Alessandro Manzoni.

Victoria, Tomás Luis de
(about 1548–1611).
Spanish composer who lived in Italy for many years (and for this reason is sometimes known as Vittoria). He wrote only church music, and its deeply devotional character is often compared with the music of Palestrina, whom he knew in Rome.

Villa-Lobos, Heitor (1887–1959).
Brazilian pianist and the most famous Latin American composer. He wrote a very large amount of music: operas, ballets, symphonies, concertos, and the well-known *Bachianas Brasileiras*, which are pieces for various instrumental and vocal groups combining something of the spirit of Bach with traditional Brazilian songs and dances. He also composed some very imaginative and beautiful music for the guitar.

Vitry, Philippe de (1291–1361).
French poet, priest, court official and composer. Only a few examples of his music survive, but he has a significant place in musical history on account of his treatise explaining new styles of composition which he was probably the first to call *ars nova*, or the 'New Art'.

Vivaldi, Antonio
(about 1678–1741).
Italian priest, violinist and composer who spent much of his life teaching music at a girls' orphanage in Venice, though he died in Vienna. He built upon the work of his older compatriots Corelli and Torelli, writing well over four hundred works in the concerto grosso style, the most famous of these being his very descriptive set of four concertos with a part for solo violin called *The Four*

Richard Wagner

Seasons. Known as 'The Red Priest' because of the colour of his hair, Vivaldi also composed operas and oratorios. Bach admired and arranged some of his music.

Wagner, Richard (1813–83).
German composer, born in Leipzig, who revolutionized opera, orchestration and harmony, and also strongly influenced the artistic and philosophical thought of his time. His greatest single aim was the creation of what he considered a new art

form called 'music drama'. By force of will, and with other people's money, he achieved his ambitions, also planning and seeing built a special theatre for his operas and music-dramas at Bayreuth in Bavaria. His second wife Cosima (Liszt's daughter, who divorced the conductor Hans von Bülow to marry him) and their two sons presided over the Bayreuth Festival until well into this century. Wagner himself died in Venice. His early operas include *Rienzi* (in its original version the

Fats Waller

longest of all his single operas but not typical of his subsequent work), *Der fliegende Holländer* ('The Flying Dutchman'), *Tannhäuser* (based on the life of a medieval German minstrel-knight) and *Lohengrin* (inspired by legends of the Holy Grail). After that he started work on what turned out to be his greatest realization of music drama: *Der Ring des Nibelungen* ('The Ring of the Nibelungs'), a cycle of four operas based on Teutonic myths and legends—*Das Rheingold* ('The Rhinegold'), *Die Walküre* ('The Valkyries'), *Siegfried* and *Götterdämmerung* ('Twilight of the Gods'). The other music dramas of his maturity are *Tristan und Isolde* (a love story from Celtic legend), *Die Meistersinger von Nürnberg* ('The

Mastersingers of Nuremberg', an evocation of the art and culture of Renaissance Germany), and *Parsifal* (based on another aspect of the Holy Grail legends, Parsifal being Lohengrin's father). A popular orchestral piece is the *Siegfried Idyll*, based on music from the opera *Siegfried*, which Wagner composed to celebrate the birth of his son— Siegfried!

Waller, Thomas Wright 'Fats'
(1904–43).
American jazz pianist and songwriter. 'Fats' Waller was one of the most colourful and entertaining figures in jazz, a large man almost always pictured with a bowler hat perched jauntily on his head. He was a fine pianist with an immaculate

sense of swing, at his best accompanying himself in some of the songs that helped to make him famous— 'Honeysuckle Rose' and 'Ain't Misbehavin'. The son of a church minister, he also sometimes played the organ or harmonium in a clever jazz style.

Walther von der Vogelweide
(about 1170–1230).
Greatest of the medieval German poet-musicians known as *Minnesinger* ('Singers of Love'), whose songs were generally more serious and scholarly than those of the troubadours and *trouvères* of Provence and France. He is portrayed in Wagner's opera *Tannhäuser*, which is the story of another German poet-musician or minstrel-knight of the Middle Ages.

Sir William Walton—portrait by Michael Ayrton

Walton, Sir William (1902–83).
English composer, not so interested
in English folk music and literature
as Vaughan Williams and Britten,
developing instead a strong, bright
orchestral style and sometimes
influenced by jazz. His works include
Façade (originally composed to
accompany poems by Edith Sitwell,
now better known either as a ballet or
as a full-scale orchestral suite), two
symphonies, the concert overtures
Portsmouth Point and *Scapino*, the
opera *Troilus and Cressida*, and the
oratorio *Belshazzar's Feast*; also film
music.

Weber, Carl Maria von
(1786–1826).
German conductor and composer.
His operas *Der Freischütz* ('The
Marksman'), *Euryanthe* and *Oberon*
were very important in the development of German Romantic opera,
and influenced Wagner. He also
wrote some fine orchestral and
instrumental music, notably for the
clarinet, and the well-known
Invitation to the Dance (originally a
piano piece, later orchestrated by
Berlioz). Like Chopin he had poor
health and died relatively young
from consumption.

Webern, Anton von (1883–1945).
Austrian composer. Together with
Alban Berg, he was Schoenberg's
principal musical disciple, developing
his own style based on twelve-tone
methods of composition. The outstanding feature of his style is
extreme brevity and economy of
notes, great significance being
attached to every single note or sound
in a piece. His actual compositions
are also few in number, but of
importance to twentieth-century
music. They can be regarded as the
final and complete reaction against
the massive late Romantic orchestral

works of Mahler, Richard Strauss and others. Webern was accidentally shot dead by an Allied soldier at the end of the Second World War.

Weelkes, Thomas
(about 1575–1623).
English organist and composer of church music, some instrumental pieces for viols, and many madrigals. With other Elizabethan madrigalists he contributed to *The Triumphs of Oriana*.

Weill, Kurt (1900–50).
German composer who settled in the United States after the Nazi rise to power. His fame rests with the satiri-cal, jazz-style operas he produced in collaboration with the dramatist Berthold Brecht—*Die Drei-groschenoper* ('The Threepenny Opera', being an adaptation of the eighteenth-century English stage piece *The Beggar's Opera*), and *The Rise and Fall of the City of Mahagonny*. The well-known song 'Mack the Knife' comes from the first of these.

Wilbye, John (1574–1638).
English composer of some of the finest madrigals of the Elizabethan period, contributing to the famous collection published as *The Triumphs of Oriana*. He composed very little else.

Willaert, Adriaan
(about 1490–1562).
Flemish composer who was Director of Music at St Mark's, Venice. In this capacity he created the antiphonal styles of music—contrasting one group of singers or instrumentalists with another—which Andrea and Giovanni Gabrieli developed further and which made Venice such an influential centre of Renaissance and early Baroque music. He also com-posed some of the first true madrigals.

Williamson, Malcolm (born 1931).
Australian composer who has worked mainly in Britain. His works include the opera *Our Man in Havana* (based on Graham Greene's satirical novel about the Secret Service) and the large-scale choral and orchestral Mass of Christ the King.

Wolf, Hugo (1860–1903).
Austrian composer, mainly of songs which are considered among the finest in the tradition of German Romantic *Lieder*. There are three important groups of these, *The Italian Song Book*, *The Spanish Song Book* and the *Mörike Songs* (to words by the German poet G.F. Mörike). Other songs are to poems by Goethe. Wolf also wrote one opera, *Der Corregidor* (set in Spain), and the *Italian Serenade* for string quartet (which he later orchestrated). He died insane.

Xenakis, Iannis (born 1922).
Greek composer who has introduced many new ideas into music, includ-ing the use of mathematical formulae and computers in composition.

Ysaÿe, Eugène (1858–1931).
World-famous Belgian violinist, also a conductor and composer mainly of concertos and other works for the violin.

Carl Maria von Weber

Musical Forms and Terms

Absolute Music
Music that is supposed to express no thought or idea beyond the music itself; the exact opposite of descriptive programme music.

Absolute Pitch (or Perfect Pitch)
The ability to identify the PITCH of a note or the KEY of a piece of music by ear alone.

Accelerando
Italian tempo marking, meaning 'accelerate, speed up'.

Accidental
The sharpening or flattening of a particular note not accounted for in the KEY signature of a piece; or the temporary naturalizing of a note that is sharpened or flattened according to the key signature.

Adagio
Italian tempo marking, meaning 'slow'. Thus *adagio maestoso*, 'slow and majestic'.

Aleatory
Derived from the Latin word *alea* meaning 'dice', it describes music in which the composer has introduced an element of chance into the performance. The term is often taken to include music that invites the performers to decide for themselves when and at what point in the score to start or stop playing, though strictly speaking this is a matter of *indeterminacy* and not quite the same.

Allegro
Italian tempo marking, meaning 'fairly fast'. Thus *allegro con brio*, 'fairly fast and with spirit'; *allegro ma non troppo*, 'steady and not too fast'. *Allegretto* means 'little allegro', or 'not quite so fast'.

Alto
1) The range of pitch of a boy's voice, deeper than treble, or the pitch of a man's voice singing falsetto (a counter-tenor);
2) the range of pitch of an instrument within a particular family of instruments (e.g. alto saxophone);
3) the name of a CLEF.

Andante
Italian tempo marking, meaning 'at a leisurely pace'. Thus *andante cantabile*, 'leisurely and in a singing style'.

Anthem
1) A piece of church choral music dating back in name and style to the establishment of the Church of England and taking the place of the older Roman Catholic Latin MOTET;
2) any fairly solemn piece of choral or vocal music, like national anthems.

Antiphonal
From the Greek word meaning 'sounding across', it describes music intended to be performed by separate groups of singers or instrumentalists so as to produce a kind of stereophonic effect. An *antiphon* is a piece of church music that usually includes alternative passages for a solo singer and a whole choir, or alternative passages for two separate choirs.

Arco
Italian for 'bow', telling players of stringed instruments to start using their bows again after playing PIZZICATO.

Aria
Italian for 'song', mainly used to describe the fairly substantial and often technically difficult songs of opera and oratorio.

Arpeggio
From the Italian *arpa*, 'harp', it describes the method of spreading out the notes of a chord one after the other, almost always from the bottom note upwards, as they are usually played on the harp.

Atonal Music
Music not written in any of the major or minor keys. Some of Wagner's music verges on atonality; pioneer figures of twentieth-century music, such as Debussy and Bartók, also developed atonal styles of composition; but the term is most closely associated with Schoenberg's TWELVE-TONE methods of compostion.

Aubade
French for a 'morning song'; *alborado* is the equivalent Spanish word sometimes used.

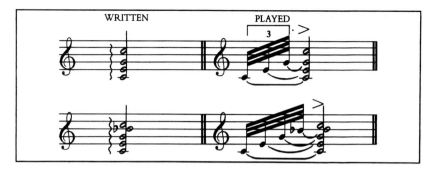

Chords to be played in an arpeggio style are written with a wavy line against them, as shown. This example also shows how to play them.

Ayre
English name for a type of song dating from about the end of the sixteenth century. The more up-to-date spelling is *air*.

Bagatelle
French word meaning 'trifle', and a name for fairly short, not too weighty pieces of music, usually for the piano; but Beethoven's bagatelles are more than just trifles.

Ballad
Type of song usually connected with a narrative poem (i.e. a poem recounting a story). Many traditional ballads are folk songs dating back, in various forms, hundreds of years. A *ballade*, the French version of the word, was used by Chopin and others as a title for piano pieces of a vaguely descriptive character.

Ballet
Combination of music and dancing. Examples of this can be found in most tribal societies, while in the ancient world the Greeks sometimes included dancing and music as a part of their drama. But ballet as we think of it today originated in Renaissance Italy and reached its first period of artistic importance in seventeenth-century France, at the court of Louis XIV. *Opéra-ballet* was basically opera with ballet sequences (a feature of much French opera), while *ballet-pantomime* was closer to true ballet, with no singing. Thus the traditional home of ballet is France, and though some of the finest ballet companies and ballet scores have been Russian, the names of the various dance steps and other technical terms are all in French. *Choreography* is the art of planning and creating ballet steps and routines, and the choreographer is the most important person in any ballet production. Some famous ballets (e.g. *Coppélia, Swan Lake, The Nutcracker, Petrushka, The Three-Cornered Hat*) have had music specially written for them. Others (e.g. *Les Sylphides, Façade, Pineapple Poll*) have music taken from some other source.

Bar
A small section of music. Most Western music is divided up into bars according to a regular rhythmic beat, though it is quite possible to change the rhythm from one bar to the next. The American name is *measure*.

Barcarolle
French word for a boating song, especially associated with Venetian gondolas. Chopin and Offenbach (in *The Tales of Hoffmann*) wrote bar-carolles.

Baritone
1) The range of pitch of a man's voice, deeper than TENOR, not so deep as BASS;
2) the range of pitch of an instrument within a particular family of instruments (e.g. baritone saxophone).

Bass
1) The deepest range of pitch of a man's voice;
2) the deepest-pitched type of instrument within a particular family of instruments (e.g. bass viol);
3) the name of a CLEF.

Bel Canto
Italian for 'beautiful song', describing an operatic style of singing originally concerned with a refined and beautiful vocal tone, but meaning also singing of great agility and control.

Bebop
Jazz style which led to most other modern or 'progressive' jazz styles. The name (sometimes shortened to bop) suggests the generally restless, urgent character of the music.

Berceuse
French name for a lullaby or cradle song, given to some instrumental pieces.

Blues
Early and basic jazz style, a type of sung lament divided into sections of twelve bars with set harmonies. Other jazz, dance and pop music forms have developed from it. Composers and song-writers have loosely applied the name to pieces of a general jazz-like character.

Boogie Woogie
Jazz piano style like a kind of speeded-up Blues with a strong OSTINATO left-hand part.

Breve
Name for what was originally the note of briefest duration, but is today the note of longest duration and rarely used. The American name is *double-whole-note*.

Cadence
A kind of harmonic punctuation mark, usually consisting of two chords. According to the established rules of harmony, some types of cadence bring a piece of music to a

satisfactory close (like the *plagal cadence* which forms the 'amen' at the end of hymns), while others lead the music in new directions.

Cadenza

The Italian word for 'cadence', which also describes the section of a concerto movement reserved for the soloist. Originally the composer usually left a gap in the music, during which the soloist was supposed to improvize upon the tunes already heard; but most soloists today plan their cadenzas ahead of performance. In any event, since Beethoven many concertos have had their cadenzas written in by the composer.

Canon

A type of composition, rather like a ROUND, in which each voice or instrumental part enters in turn with the same melody, following each other round until the piece is brought to a satisfactory end.

Cantata

From the Italian *cantare* 'to sing', a composition for voices, usually with orchestra. Cantatas may be for a choir, for a choir and soloists or, more rarely, for one or two soloists only. They may be religious or secular.

Canticle

Type of religious hymn with words taken from the Bible except the Psalms.

Canzona

Type of medieval Italian poem and musical settings of it; but also the name sometimes given to an instrumental piece. *Canzonet* or *canzonetta*, 'little canzona', is a light and easy kind of song.

Capriccio

Italian for 'fancy' or 'whim', describing a generally light-hearted or delicately written piece of music. The French word is *caprice*.

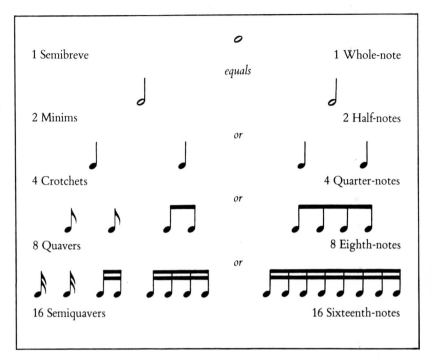

The relative duration of notes. From semibreve down to semiquaver, each type of note is equal to half the duration of the one above.

Carol

Religious song for ordinary people to sing, as opposed to trained singers; now mainly associated with Christmas, though there are carols for other festivals.

Cavatina

Italian word for a fairly short operatic aria; also sometimes applied to a song-like instrumental piece.

Chaconne

Originally a courtly dance, better known as a type of composition in variation form, in which a simple theme or motif repeated in the bass (called a ground bass) provides a basis for variations. Chaconnes may be vocal, but the form is best known as an instrumental one.

Chamber Music (Room Music)

The term grew up during the seventeenth and eighteenth centuries to describe instrumental music for small groups of players intended for the more informal atmosphere of a private room than for church, opera house or other public place. Though it has kept this meaning, it more specially describes the smaller instrumental forms that developed during the Classical period of the eighteenth century—the trio (piano, violin, cello), string quartet, string quintet and similar groups. By convention, music for one or two instruments is not usually classed as chamber music. We speak of a chamber music concert, but of a piano or violin recital.

Chanson

French for 'song', especially the name for a type of medieval or Renaissance French song for one or more voices, perhaps with instruments.

Charleston

Lively type of dance, developed out of early jazz, that was very popular in the United States and Europe during the 1920s.

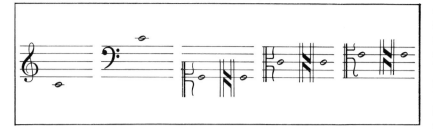

The five clefs, showing how each is related to the same note, middle C. The treble and bass clefs are the most familiar ones today.

Chorale
Traditional type of German hymn tune, specially associated with the Lutheran Church. A *chorale-prelude* is an instrumental piece, usually for the organ, based on a chorale tune.

Chord
Two or more notes of different pitch sounded together.

Chromatic Scale
Progression of notes going up or down in pitch by a SEMITONE between each note, and therefore different from any of the major or minor scales. Obtained on a piano by playing both the white and black keys in succession.

Clef
In staff notation the sign that governs the pitch of notes written on or between the STAVE lines. There are five clefs, SOPRANO, TREBLE, ALTO, TENOR and BASS. The treble and bass clefs are the most widely used.

Coda
Italian for 'tail', describing an extra passage of music added to the end of a piece to round it off.

Coloratura
Italian word describing, usually in the case of a SOPRANO, a singer with a specially agile voice.

Concerto
Italian word for an orchestral composition with a major part for one, two or possibly three instrumental soloists.

The Classical concerto of Mozart's time had three movements, and with only a few exceptions this arrangement has been followed since. A *concerto for orchestra*, of which there are several examples this century, gives prominence to each instrumental group in the orchestra in turn.

Concerto Grosso
Italian for 'great concerto', an earlier form than the true concerto, most often composed for a string orchestra and a smaller group of string soloists, passages for the full orchestra (*ripieno*, 'replenished' or 'full') being contrasted with those for the soloists (*concertino*, 'little concert' or 'little group').

Conductus
Early type of POLYPHONIC composition for a choir. One singer declaimed a *cantus firmus* (Latin, 'fixed song'), around which the other parts were added. The origin of the name may be connected with religious processions, when priests, or effigies, were conducted from place to place.

Consort
Performance by a group of instrumentalists all playing instruments of the same family, e.g. viols or recorders, very popular in Renaissance times. A *broken consort* combined stringed and wind instruments.

Continuo
A continuous musical part in a work, usually for a keyboard instrument, designed to provide a lead or foundation to the performance; especially associated with seventeenth- and eighteenth-century orchestral music, but used also in some types of opera to aid the singers in RECITATIVE. Very often composers of the period in question directed performances of their own music by taking the continuo part. A *figured bass* was a kind of coded notation for continuo players, the figures indicating what chords and harmonies to play.

Contralto
The range of pitch of a woman's voice, deeper than SOPRANO.

Counterpoint
From the Latin *punctus contra punctum*, 'point against point' or 'note against note', a form of POLYPHONIC music in which two or more melodies, or different versions of the same melody, are played against each other, or interwoven note by note. The FUGUE is the greatest form of contrapuntal music.

Courante
French courtly dance, often used as the basis for a movement in eighteenth-century suites and other instrumental and orchestral music.

Crescendo (cresc.)
Italian dynamic marking, meaning 'get gradually louder'.

Crotchet
Note of duration, now used as the basis for many kinds of rhythm and tempo; the duration of other notes are usually measured against it. The American name is *quarter-note*.

Diatonic Music
Music written in one or other of the twenty-four major or minor keys; that is, most music written between about 1600 and 1900.

Diminuendo (dim.)
Italian dynamic marking, meaning 'get gradually softer'.

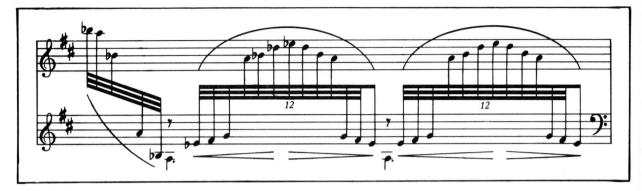

Dynamic markings in a passage from Debussy's Piano Prelude *Ondine*. Within each group of notes the music gets louder and softer again, as indicated.

Divertimento
Italian 'amusement', describing a fairly light and entertaining piece of instrumental music, usually in several movements. *Divertissement* is the French word.

Dodecaphonic Music
Greek word for TWELVE-TONE music, the method of composing, using all twelve notes of the CHROMATIC SCALE, invented by Schoenberg.

Dumka
A type of Slavonic song with alternative slow and sad, fast and happy, sections.

Duo
Music for two performers, usually referring to instrumentalists; but *duet* often means a song for two vocalists.

Dynamics
Aspect of musical performance concerned with degrees of loudness and softness.

Étude
French for 'study', a piece of instrumental music usually concerned with some aspect of playing technique.

Expressionism
Term mainly used in painting, but sometimes applied to music which is supposed to express the composer's inner or subconscious state of mind, as distinct from normal emotions. Some of Mahler's and Schoenberg's music could be called expressionist.

Fado
Type of Portuguese folk music.

Fandango
Lively Spanish dance, including castanets.

Fantasy
Name for a piece of music relatively free from any particular form and suggesting a mood of improvization. *Fantasia* and *fantaisie* are the respective Italian and French versions of the word.

Farandole
Old type of dance from Provence in southern France, traditionally for pipe and drum. Bizet's well-known farandole from his incidental music to *L'Arlésienne* is not in the correct rhythm, but is based on an old Provençal tune.

Flamenco
Type of Spanish song from Andalusia. There are various local styles, named after towns and cities of the region, e.g. the *Malagueña* and the *Sevillana*. One of the origins of flamenco is an old type of Spanish singing called *cante hondo* ('deep song'), rather sorrowful in character. The Arabic sound to the music also reminds us that Spain was occupied by the Moors of North Africa for hundreds of years.

Flat
Sign indicating that a note must be lowered in pitch by a SEMITONE.

Form
The way in which a piece of music is arranged or presented, based on many different factors, taken singly or in combination. The most important of these deal with the order in which tunes and other musical ideas are presented, the length of sections or of the whole piece reckoned in terms of bars or measures, the use of harmony, the use of rhythm. Form can also describe particular styles or methods of composition, such as the FUGUE or PASSACAGLIA.

Forte (f)
Italian dynamic marking, meaning 'loud'. *Fortissimo* (ff) means 'very loud'. *Mezzo-forte* (mf) means 'half loud', i.e. 'not too loud'.

Foxtrot
Type of American ballroom dance, very loosely based on jazz, which was popular both in America and Europe during the 1920s and 1930s.

Frequency
Term in the science of acoustics for the speed or rapidity of vibrations

giving rise to sound waves.
Frequency is expressed in terms of the
number of vibrations per second. It is
directly related to PITCH, as any
simple experiment with a stretched
piece of string or elastic will show—
the faster or higher the frequency, the
higher the pitch of the sound.

Frottola
Italian song for several voices dating
from about the beginning of the
sixteenth century, and an early
version of the MADRIGAL.

Fugue
The most developed form of
COUNTERPOINT, in which a theme is
first stated on its own, then added to
in one or more versions or 'parts', and
so built up into a closely interwoven
musical structure. Bach and other
composers of the Baroque period
wrote fugues which were compositions in their own right. Later composers, notably Beethoven, sometimes included a type of fugue as part
of a larger movement in a symphony,
string quartet, sonata or other composition. The Italian term *fugato*
means in a generally fugal style rather
than a true fugue.

Galliard
Lively court dance of the fifteenth
and sixteenth centuries.

Gavotte
Old type of dance sometimes included in instrumental suites of
dances.

Glee
Type of English song for men's
voices, popular in England during the
eighteenth century, and then in the
United States.

Gopak
Lively Russian folk dance.

Grave
Italian expression of mood, 'grave,
solemn', often also meaning a slow
tempo.

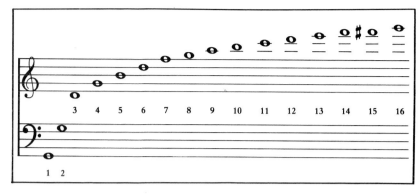

Harmonic series of a note. The fundamental, or leading note, is the lower G in the bass
clef. The second harmonic is the G an octave above, the third is the D at an interval of a
fifth above. The series continues upwards in pitch by progressively shorter intervals.

Harmonics (or Harmonic series)
The notes of different pitch that
blend in various ways to make up any
normal musical note, created by the
fact that a vibrating string or column
of air vibrates not only as a whole but
in parts. The first and usually dom-
inating note in a harmonic series is
called the *fundamental*. The rest are
overtones, or *upper partials*.

Harmony
That aspect of music concerned with
blending notes and sequences of notes
of different pitch.

Impromptu
Short instrumental piece, usually for
the piano, in an improvizatory style.

Improvization
The art of composing music spontaneously. In the past it often meant
improvizing on an existing theme, as

Bach did, or improvizing on the
themes of a concerto movement in
the CADENZA section reserved for the
soloist. Much JAZZ is also improvized,
within the framework of a form like
the BLUES, or on the basis of a given
tune.

Incidental Music
Music written in connection with a
play or other stage work, to be played
before, during and perhaps at the
close of the performance. Much
incidental music becomes best known
in the concert hall in the form of
overtures and suites.

Intermezzo
Italian for 'between' or 'in the middle', describing a piece of orchestral
music to be played between the
scenes of an opera; occasionally the
name given to a short piece of
instrumental music.

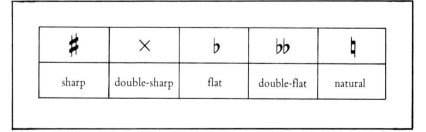

♯	×	♭	♭♭	♮
sharp	double-sharp	flat	double-flat	natural

The signs for sharp, flat and natural. Double-sharp indicates the raising in pitch of a
note by a whole tone; double-flat indicates the lowering in pitch of a note by the same
tonal interval.

Interval

The 'distance' in pitch between two notes.

Invention

Name used by Bach for fairly short keyboard pieces, more fully called *two-part inventions* because they use two 'parts' or melodic lines in a contrapuntal way.

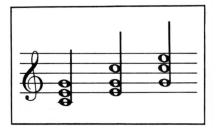

Simple chord inversions. Harmonically the chord remains the same, but the arrangement of the individual notes changes.

Inversion

1) A change in the placing of notes in a chord, according to pitch;
2) a melody played 'upside down', that is, with the relative pitch intervals between the notes reversed.

Jazz

The music primarily of black Americans, though there are many white jazz musicians also. Early or basic jazz forms—BLUES, RAGTIME, STOMPS, BOOGIE—are characterized by strong, syncopated rhythms (related to Latin American music), particular chords and harmonic sequences, and a large measure of IMPROVIZATION. Jazz later developed forms and styles, notably BEBOP, that considerably changed its original character. It also led to many dance music styles—SWING, ROCK N' ROLL.

Jig

A lively dance, associated especially with rural Britain. Under its French title of *gigue* it often forms a movement of instrumental dance suites.

American vocalist Ella Fitzgerald who has done much to popularize jazz singing. She is a noted scat singer (see page 184).

Jive

A very energetic way of dancing to swing and other jazz-inspired types of dance music.

Key

1) The most important factor in the HARMONY of much Western music written between about 1600 and the present day. The key to a piece of music is any one of the twenty-four major or minor SCALES on which the music is based; the *key-signature* at the beginning of a printed piece of music indicates which notes, if any, must be sharpened or flattened for the piece to conform to a particular scale. Changes of key mean moving the music from the harmonic context of one scale to another;
2) a lever which controls the mechanism for making one particular note sound in instruments like the piano and organ; the complete set of such keys forms a keyboard.

Ländler

Type of Austrian country dance, like a slow WALTZ. Mahler based some of his symphonic movements upon it.

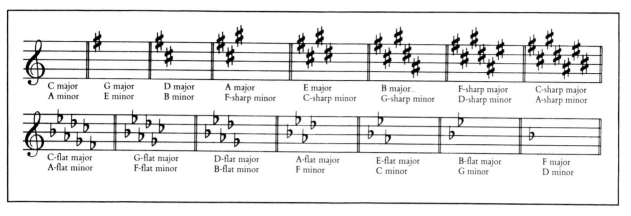

Key-signatures for the twenty-four major and minor keys. Each signature represents a major and its relative minor key.

Largo

Italian for 'broad', which can be a definite tempo marking for 'slow and stately', or indicate a mood corresponding to this. It is not really the name for a type of composition, despite Handel's 'Largo' (which he did not compose as such). *Larghetto*, 'little largo' meaning not quite so slow .

Ledger Line

In NOTATION, a short line or lines added above or below the normal stave lines to accommodate notes of extra high or low pitch.

Legato

Italian for 'bound together', describing a manner of performance whereby the notes are played without any sort of break to create a smooth, flowing effect.

Lento

Italian tempo marking, meaning 'slow'.

Lied

See SONG.

Lullaby

A cradle-song, to make a baby sleep.

Madrigal

Italian name for a type of part-song (i.e. polyphonic in style) for a small group of singers, very popular during the Renaissance period, first in Italy, then in England. Most madrigals were secular pieces, but a few were religious.

Magnificat

Religious choral work, basically a setting of the Hymn of the Virgin Mary, sometimes built up into a substantial composition, as by Bach, for chorus, soloists and orchestra.

March

Basically a type of military music for marching to; but slow or funeral marches have formed the basis for some slow movements in symphonies and sonatas.

Masque

Type of stage entertainment with some singing and dancing, related to opera; popular in England during the seventeenth century. The term has occasionally been used since.

Mass

Principal service of the Roman Catholic Church which has been set to music by composers of many different times, and in many different styles. The version usually set to music is known as the 'Ordinary' of the Mass, and consists of five sections—*Kyrie eleison* (Greek 'Lord, have mercy'), *Gloria in excelsis Deo* (Latin 'Glory to God on high'), *Credo* (Latin 'I believe'), *Sanctus* and *Benedictus* (Latin 'Holy' and 'Blessed'), *Agnus Dei* (Latin 'Lamb of God'). The Latin word *Missa* is sometimes used, as in *Missa Solemnis* ('Solemn Mass') and *Missa Brevis* ('Short Mass'). The *Requiem Mass* is a special form of the service, in memory of the dead (*Requiem* means 'repose').

Mazurka

Polish country dance, used by Chopin as the basis for many piano pieces.

Melody

An organized progression of notes of varying pitch, almost always shaped by matters of rhythm and duration; as distinct from HARMONY.

Minuet

Originally a country dance and then a court dance, with three beats to the bar. It was the basis of many movements in eighteenth-century instrumental suites; also formed the basis for the third movement in most symphonies and string quartets of the Classical period.

Minim

Note of duration, equal to two CROTCHETS. The American name is *half-note*.

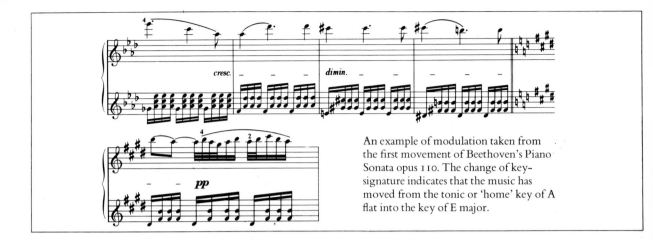

An example of modulation taken from the first movement of Beethoven's Piano Sonata opus 110. The change of key-signature indicates that the music has moved from the tonic or 'home' key of A flat into the key of E major.

Mode
1) Name for each of the SCALES, of Greek origin, which provided the basis for much European music from about the sixth until the sixteenth century;
2) name sometimes given to major and minor scales.

Modulation
To change harmonically from one KEY to another in the course of a single piece of music.

Morris
English folk dance, traditionally played by pipe and drum. The dancers themselves wear bells.

Motet
Type of church choral composition, polyphonic in style, set to religious texts in Latin, and one of the principal forms of composition from about the tenth to the sixteenth century. Since then the name has been given to a much wider variety of compositions, but still nearly always religious in character.

Mute
Device to soften the sound of an instrument, and which almost always modifies its tone as well. In the case of stringed instruments mutes are small clamps placed over the strings at the bridge; with brass instruments they are objects placed in the bell.

Natural
1) In staff NOTATION the sign cancelling previous instructions to sharpen or flatten a note;
2) name sometimes given to a brass wind instrument that has no valves or other mechanical device and so can play only notes belonging to its 'natural' harmonics.

Nocturne
'Night piece', usually a piano piece of a generally quiet, reflective character. This style of nocturne was introduced by the Irish composer John Field, but made famous by Chopin. A few other composers have since used the term.

Nonet
Piece for nine performers, singers or instrumentalists.

Notation
Any system of writing music down, including the TONIC-SOL-FA and TABLATURE, but normally taken to mean the system based on staff lines or STAVES. Here sets of lines across the page (now five in number) provide the framework for the placing of notes on or between the lines, above or below them, as indications of pitch. The exact pitch of the notes is qualified by CLEF, KEY and the use of ACCIDENTALS. Rhythm is indicated by BARS, setting out the measure of the music, and the relative value of notes in terms of duration.

Obbligato
Italian for 'obligatory' or 'compulsory', originally meaning that a part in a piece of music was compulsory; but now sometimes meaning almost the exact opposite, e.g. an instrumental obbligato part to accompany a singer being taken to mean that it is optional.

Octave (8vo)
From the Latin *octo*, 'eight', with reference to the eight notes that make up any major or minor scale. In acoustics any note sounded an exact octave above another has twice the FREQUENCY.

Octet
Piece for eight performers, singers or instrumentalists.

Opera
The word is the plural of the Latin *opus*, 'a work'. It describes the type of musical stage drama that originated in Italy in the early seventeenth century. Basically, most opera consists of dialogue between the singers, interspersed by songs or choruses. In traditional Italian *opera seria* ('serious' or 'tragic opera') and *opera buffa* ('comic opera') the dialogue is declaimed in a special singing style called RECITATIVE; in other kinds of opera, German *singspiel* and French *opéra-comique* (which is not necessarily comic) it is spoken. Wagner dispensed with all

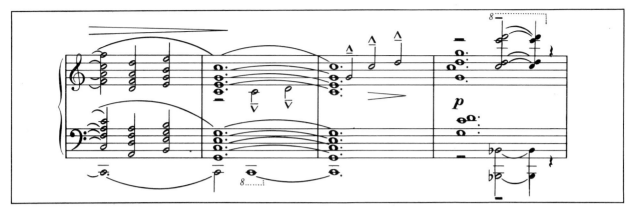

Use of octave signs in Debussy's Piano Prelude *La Cathédrale engloutie*. The notes or chords encompassed by the dotted line are played either an octave lower or higher than written. Note also the tie lines extending the duration of the chords.

such traditions, creating a continuous flow of music, shared between singers and orchestra, which he called 'music-drama'.

Operetta
Italian for 'little opera', describing a much lighter kind of entertainment than true opera, which grew up during the nineteenth century and led to musical comedy and to many stage and film musicals.

Oratorio
Traditionally a kind of religious opera, but without stage action or costumes, owing its name to the fact that the earliest known examples of oratorio were performed in the Oratory of St Philip Neri, Rome, in the early seventeenth century. Today there are some secular choral and vocal works called oratorios, though still of a generally serious and moral character.

Organum
Early form of *polyphony* (i.e. vocal music with two or more melodic lines or 'parts') which grew directly out of PLAINSONG, dating from about the tenth century.

Opus
Latin for 'work', used a great deal in the publication of music, to identify a composition or group of compo-

sitions. The opus numbers given to many seventeenth- and eighteenth-century works may have little connection with their actual order of composition. From the time of Beethoven, they usually do.

Ostinato
Italian for 'obstinate', describing a musical phrase that is repeated over and over again, usually as a form of accompaniment. In jazz BOOGIE uses a very destinctive type of ostinato.

Overture
From the French *ouverture* meaning 'opening', describing a piece of orchestral music played at the opening, i.e. the beginning, of many operas and other stage works. In the nineteenth century the word also began to be applied to short orchestral pieces, usually with some kind of descriptive 'programme' but not connected with any larger stage work. These are known as concert overtures.

Part
An individual melodic line in a piece of music written in a generally polyphonic style. So a four-part FUGUE means a fugue built up on four melodic lines. A *part-song* is one that is made up of individual melodic lines, like a MADRIGAL.

Partita
Italian name for a SUITE in the seventeenth- and eighteenth-century sense of a group of instrumental pieces generally in dance style. Occasionally it can describe a piece in the form of a theme and variations.

Pasadoble
Type of Spanish dance, the word meaning 'double step'.

Passacaglia
An old court dance that developed into a type of composition consisting of variations built upon a constantly repeated theme or motif. In this respect it is similar to a CHACONNE.

Passion
Choral, vocal and orchestral settings of the gospel accounts of Christ's betrayal, trial and crucifixion, similar in form and style to ORATORIO.

Pastoral
Originally the name given to a type of musical stage piece with a rustic theme or setting, but better known today as the special name or nickname given to many compositions which have some connection with the countryside.

Pavan (or Pavane)
Slow, stately court dance of the Renaissance period.

The opening of Debussy's Piano Prelude *Bruyères* ('Heather') with phrase marks indicating how the melody should be shaped, or 'flow'. Note also the various rests.

Phrase

A melodic sequence, usually part of a longer melody. *Phrasing* in a general sense means correctly interpreting the natural flow of the music. *Phrase-marks* in printed music are a guide to this.

Piano (p)

Italian dynamic marking, meaning 'soft'. *Pianissimo* (pp) means 'very soft'.

Pitch

The highness or lowness of a note according to the FREQUENCY (i.e. speed or rapidity) of its vibrations. *Concert-pitch* is the internationally agreed basis for tuning instruments, centred upon the note A above middle C, this being equal to a frequency of 440 cycles per second.

Pizzicato (pizz.)

Italian for 'pinched', but in music an indication for bowed stringed instruments that the strings must be plucked.

Plainsong (or Plainchant)

The style of unaccompanied, un-harmonized chanting used in the early Christian church and still to be heard in some Roman Catholic churches and monasteries. The best-known style of plainsong is the Gregorian Chant, named after Pope Gregory I and dating from the sixth century.

Polonaise

French word for 'Polish', describing a fairly stately type of Polish dance, which Chopin transformed into a patriotic-sounding piano piece.

Polyphony

Greek for 'many sounds' or 'many tones', describing methods of composition which involve the inter-weaving of a number of melodic lines or 'parts'. It was the basis for most Western music for hundreds of years, from about the twelfth to well into the eighteenth century.

Polyrhythm

The playing of music in several rhythms at the same time.

Polytonality

The playing of music in more than one KEY at the same time. Where only two keys are involved it can also be called *bi-tonality*.

Portamento

Italian for 'carrying', describing a style of singing or playing which carries the voice or instrument up or down from one note to the next. Excessive portamento is sometimes called 'scooping'.

Prelude

Strictly this describes a short piece of music that precedes or introduces a more substantial piece, like the prelude to some operas, or the prelude to a fugue. But Chopin and Debussy used the word to describe groups of piano pieces, each piece being self-contained in style and mood.

Presto

Italian tempo marking, meaning 'fast'. *Prestissimo*, 'very fast'.

Programme Music

Descriptive music intended either to evoke a mood or feeling, or to re-create the events of some story. Much nineteenth-century Romantic instrumental and orchestral music has some descriptive 'programme'. The term does not normally apply to opera, ballet or songs, whose music, by its very nature, must be descriptive of something.

Progressive Tonality

The practice of beginning a single piece of music, or a longer work like a symphony, in one KEY and ending in another.

Quartet

Piece for four performers, singers or instrumentalists.

Quaver

Note of duration, half the value of a CROTCHET. The American name is *eighth-note*.

Quintet

Piece for five performers, singers or instrumentalists.

Ragtime

Early jazz style, bright and energetic. Composers and song writers have loosely applied the name to some pieces with a jazz-like character.

Rallentando

Italian tempo marking, meaning 'slow down'.

Recitative

Manner of reciting words in a song-like way, but with more attention to the inflection of the words than to any musical sense of phrasing or rhythm. It usually precedes a proper song, aria or chorus in opera or oratorio. *Recitativo secco* (Italian, 'dry recitative'), as used in much eighteenth-century opera, is delivered quickly with a light instrumental accompaniment, probably a harpsichord. *Recitativo stromentato* ('instrumental recitative') is delivered in a grander style, probably with full orchestral accompaniment.

Reel

A lively kind of dance, traditional to Scotland and Ireland. The Highland Fling is a very energetic kind of Scottish reel.

Requiem

See MASS.

Rest

A period of silence in one or more instrumental or vocal parts, usually equivalent to one or more beats to a bar. Rests are indicated in printed music by signs which correspond to the various notes of duration.

Rhapsody

Name for a piece of music in a fairly free, improvizatory style. It is sometimes given to compositions which are basically a set of variations on a theme.

Rhythm

The beat or pulse of a piece of music, and the distribution of notes within that beat according to their duration.

Semibreve	Minim	Crotchet	Quaver	Semiquaver
𝅝	𝅗𝅥	𝅘𝅥	𝅘𝅥𝅮	𝅘𝅥𝅯
—	—	↾ or ⌡	𝄾	𝄿

The principal notes of duration (see page 174) and their corresponding rest signs. Rests can play a vital part in the rhythm of a piece of music.

Ricercare

Italian for 'to seek out', the name for a polyphonic type of instrumental piece usually obeying strict rules of COUNTERPOINT, belonging mainly to the seventeenth century.

Riff

Term used mainly in jazz, swing and dance music to describe a short rhythmic or melodic phrase repeated throughout a piece.

Rigaudon

Old dance from Provence that later became a more courtly French dance. The English equivalent was called a *rigadoon.*

Rock n' Roll

Type of dance music, growing out of the basic 12-bar BLUES form, but with a strong insistent rhythm, which followed SWING in popularity during the 1950s. Bill Haley and his Comets and Elvis Presley were among its greatest stars. The name is taken from the kind of dance movements that went with the music.

Romance

Name given to various pieces of instrumental or orchestral music from the eighteenth century to the present day, indicating more a mood of gentleness and charm than any particular form or style. *Romanza*, the Italian form of the word, is sometimes used.

Rondo

Italian for 'round', describing a piece of music in which one recurring theme (the *rondo theme*) is interspersed with a series of new themes (*episodes*). It is a form that has been used as the last movement of many sonatas, string quartets, symphonies and other instrumental and orchestral works of the Classical period.

Round

From the Latin *rota* 'wheel', describing a simple version of a CANON, almost always for voices, in which each vocal 'part' joins in turn, singing the same melody in the same key, all following each other round until each decides to end.

Rubato

Italian for 'robbed', describing a way of playing a piece of music with a certain degree of licence with regard to tempo and phrasing; in other words the player 'robs' some notes of a little of their true duration in order to give a little extra to others. Some rubato is necessary in the performance of most kinds of music, if it is not to sound stiff and wooden.

Rumba

Latin American, especially Cuban, dance that was very popular as a ballroom dance in the 1930s and 1940s. The rhythm of the rumba has occasionally been used by composers, notably Gershwin.

Saltarello
Italian folk dance, lively and energetic, used as the basis for the last movement of Mendelssohn's *Italian* Symphony.

Samba
Latin American dance, similar to a RUMBA.

Sarabande
Old courtly dance, originating in Spain, often included in seventeenth- and eighteenth-century instrumental suites.

Scale
From the Italian *scala* 'stairway' or 'step', describing various sequences of notes which progress step by step in PITCH and provide the basis for systems of music, i.e. music is composed from a selection of the available notes in one or other scale or groups of scales. We are most familiar with the major and minor scales, divided up into OCTAVE sections, each conforming to the same sequence of pitch intervals; but other systems of scale have been the old church MODES, each with its own special sequence of pitch intervals; the *pentatonic* scale of only five notes (corresponding in terms of pitch intervals to the black notes on a piano keyboard) which has formed the basis of much folk music in different parts of the world; and the CHROMATIC scale forming the basis of TWELVE-TONE composition.

Scat Singing
A jazz style of singing in which the voice does not sing words but imitates the rhythm and tone of other instruments. The old Celtic, especially Scottish, 'mouth music' was similar in its intentions.

Scherzo
Italian for 'joke'.
1) Describing a much speeded up and more dynamic version of the MINUET which Beethoven introduced as the third movement to most of his symphonies, and in some of his instru-

mental works;
2) the name for other fairly fast and dramatic instrumental or orchestral pieces, not necessarily in the same rhythm as the Beethoven-style scherzo.

Semibreve
Note of duration and the longest in normal use today, twice the value of the MINIM, four times that of the CROTCHET. The American name is *whole-note*.

Semiquaver
Note of duration, half the value of a QUAVER, or one quarter the value of a CROTCHET. The American name is *sixteenth-note*.

Semitone
'Half tone', the smallest interval of PITCH normally used in Western music. With reference to a piano keyboard, examples of semitones are from any note E to the adjacent F, F to F sharp, B to C.

Septet
Piece for seven performers, instrumentalists or singers.

Sequence
1) The repetition of a musical phrase at a different PITCH, probably meaning in a different KEY;
2) type of hymn in the Roman Catholic Church, its origins going back to the early days of polyphony and departure from PLAINSONG.

Serenade
'Night piece', the opposite of an AUBADE, but a name applied to many different pieces of music, usually intended as light entertainment. In the Classical period of the eighteenth century it often described an instrumental or orchestral piece of several movements, almost like a small symphony, as in Mozart's *Eine Kleine Nachtmusik* ('A Little Night Music').

Serial Music
Music based on any selected series of

notes, but applying mainly to TWELVE-TONE composition.

Sextet
Piece for six players, instrumentalists or singers.

Sforzando (sf)
Italian 'reinforced', a dynamic marking, meaning that a note or chord should be played with special emphasis.

Sharp
Sign indicating that a note must be raised in pitch by a SEMITONE.

Sinfonia
Early name for a symphony, sometimes given to overtures. In the eighteenth century a *sinfonia concertante* was a sort of cross between a symphony and concerto, an orchestral work in several movements with solo parts for a small group of instruments. *Sinfonietta*, 'little sinfonia', describing a small, light-weight symphony, sometimes used also as the name for a small orchestra.

Solmization
Any method of keeping a written record of music by the use of syllables as distinct from *staff notation*. The best-known method is the *Tonic Sol-Fa* in which the syllables doh, ray, me, fah, soh, lah, te, doh represent the order of notes in a scale and not their actual pitch. Doh (the first, or TONIC note in a scale) can stand for any chosen note, and the other notes in a simple tune, as expressed by their syllable, follow from it. Such methods, which are really memory aids, date back to the eleventh century and the ideas of Guido d'Arezzo.

Solo
Performance by one person.

Sonata
From the Italian *suonare* 'to sound', an instrumental piece originating in the seventeenth century; reaching its

best-known form in the Classical period of the eighteenth century as a composition for a solo keyboard instrument, or keyboard and one other solo instrument, usually in three movements. During the nineteenth century this form was further modified or expanded by Beethoven, Liszt and others.

Sonata Form
Special way of organizing a single piece of music which evolved during the Classical period of the eighteenth century. It is basically in three sections—Exposition (presentation of themes and other musical ideas), Development (literally meaning the development or modification of those existing themes and ideas), Recapitulation (a return to the music of the Exposition but usually with some modification as to key). Sonata form provides the basis for many first movements of instrumental sonatas, trios and string quartets, orchestral concertos and symphonies. It is sometimes applied to other movements.

Song
Vocal composition as distinct from choral, often for one voice only, but sometimes for a small group of singers, in which case it may be a part-song with a separate melodic line or part for each singer. Songs exist under many different names, e.g. CANZONA, CHANSON, AYRE, MADRIGAL. The German word *Lied* is usually applied to the great tradition of song writing among German-speaking composers of the Romantic period—Schubert, Schumann, Mendelssohn, Brahms, Wolf.

Soprano
1) Highest range in pitch of a woman's voice. *Mezzo-soprano* 'half soprano', not so high in pitch as a true soprano;
2) the name of a clef.

Sostenuto
Italian 'sustained', an instruction for music to be played smoothly.

Spiritual
Name for religious folk songs of the American Negroes as they used to live and work on the cotton plantations. Like their work songs, spirituals often took the form of solo passages followed by a chorus.

Stabat Mater
Originally a type of hymn dealing with the Virgin Mary and the Crucifixion, and the basis for larger choral compositions by several composers.

Staccato
Italian 'detached', describing the method of playing notes in a quick, detached way, indicated on printed music by a dot over the notes.

Stave (or Staff)
Name for each of the lines drawn horizontally in sets of five across music paper and forming the basis of *staff notation*. See also NOTATION.

Stomp
Early jazz style, lively and energetic.

Strophic
Name for a type of song that repeats the same music (perhaps with a little modification) for each verse or stanza of the poem which it is based upon.

Suite
From the French *suivre* 'to follow', describing:
1) an instrumental composition of the seventeenth and eighteenth centuries which was a succession of pieces based on dance forms;
2) an orchestral composition of the nineteenth and twentieth centuries which is either a shortened form of a larger score (often of a ballet), or a group of pieces usually linked by some particular idea or image.

Swing
Dance music of the 1930s and 1940s, developed from jazz and characterized by strong, syncopated rhythms.

Symphonic Poem
Type of orchestral composition, created by Liszt, which has some descriptive programme, and little to do with normal symphonic form.

Symphony
Name taken from the Greek meaning 'sounding together'. It was applied in Renaissance and Baroque times to many pieces of music for a group of instrumentalists; but during the Classical period of the eighteenth century it developed out of existing forms of operatic overture to become the most important kind of orchestral composition, usually of four movements—fairly fast (perhaps with a slow introduction), slow, minuet with a central section called a trio, and fast. Haydn perfected this form, Beethoven greatly enlarged it, and in terms of size and complexity the symphony reached its most expanded form in the works of Mahler. Originally for orchestra alone, symphonies from Beethoven onward have sometimes included a choir and vocal soloists also.

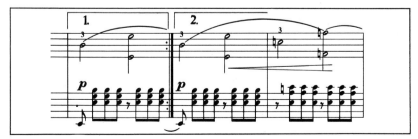

In Sonata Form, first- and second-time bars indicate when the music of the Exposition should be repeated before proceeding into the Development section (first movement of Beethoven's Piano Sonata opus 14 no 1).

129

Syncopation. This violin passage from the first movement of Beethoven's *Eroica*
Symphony clearly shows the emphasis of the beat shifting from one bar to the next.
The basic rhythm of the music is three crotchet beats to the bar.

Syncopation

Term used in rhythm to describe the
shifting of emphasis from the established beat of a piece of music,
including the placing of emphasis
between the beats of the bar. Used by
many composers, but developing its
most distinctive form in JAZZ and
SWING.

Tablature

Type of NOTATION, usually applied to
stringed instruments, that instructs
the player by symbols or diagrams
where to place his fingers in order to
obtain the required notes or chords.
Tablature was used in Renaissance
times for lutenists, and is mainly used
today for the guitar.

Tango

Latin American dance rhythm, originating in Argentina, which became
tremendously popular as a form of
ballroom dancing in Europe and the
United States during the 1920s.

Tarantella

Fast and lively dance from southern
Italy, associated both with the town
of Taranto and the tarantula spider.
The dance was supposed either to be
caused by the creature's bite or to be
a cure for it.

Te Deum

More fully in Latin *Te Deum
laudamus* ('We praise thee, O God'),
the basis for important choral works.

Temperament

Word to describe methods of tuning,
especially in connection with keyboard instruments and their ability to
play in all the major and minor keys.

Tempo

Italian for 'time', but the word is
more often concerned with the pace
or speed of a piece of music rather
than time in terms of rhythmic beats
to the bar.

Tenor

Word derived from the Latin *tenere*
'to hold', because in some polyphonic music the main melodic line
was taken or 'held' by a high-voiced
male singer. It now describes:
1) the highest-pitched range of men's
voices;
2) the range of pitch of a particular
instrument among a family of
instruments, e.g. tenor saxophone;
3) the name of a clef.

Timbre

see TONE.

Time-signature

In NOTATION, the indication of the
basic rhythm of a bar or bars within a
piece of music. It looks like an arith-
metical fraction. The top figure gives
the number of beats to the bar, the
bottom figure indicates how the beats
should be measured, e.g. as
CROTCHETS, QUAVERS, MINIMS or
other notes of duration.

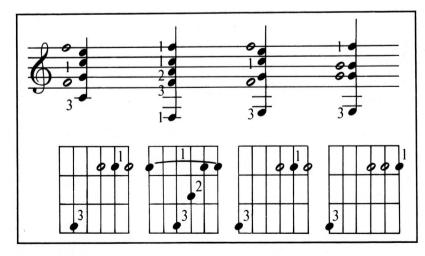

Tablature for the guitar showing finger positions on the fret-board to obtain each
chord. Numbers indicate which finger to use on each string. Circles indicate an 'open'
(i.e. unstopped) string.

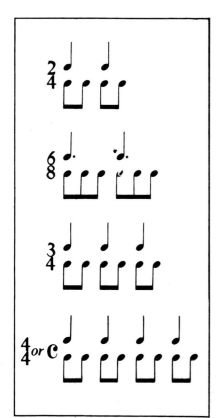

Three familiar time-signatures: two crotchets to the bar: six quavers to the bar; three crotchets to the bar (minuet and waltz time); four crotchets to the bar (or Common Time, marked C).

Toccata
From the Italian *toccare* 'to touch', describing a piece of keyboard music basically designed to test the player's finger control and touch.

Tone
1) The quality of a musical sound, also called by the French word *timbre*; 2) the pitch interval between two adjacent notes as placed on a piano keyboard, i.e. whole-tone or SEMITONE; 3) the usual American name for a note.

Tonic
The first, or leading note in any of the major or minor scales, giving its name to the scale in question. The word is also sometimes used to refer to the KEY in which a piece of music is written, especially when the music has modulated out of the tonic, or home key and then returns to it. The *tonic sol-fa* is a system for learning a melody by memorizing the relationship between the notes rather than their individual pitch. See SOLMIZATION.

Transcription
To make a new instrumental or vocal arrangement of a piece of music. There are many famous transcriptions, including J.S. Bach's arrangement for four harpsichords of Vivaldi's Concerto for Four Violins, Leopold Stokowski's orchestral transcription of Bach's Organ Toccata and Fugue in D minor, and Ravel's orchestral version of Mussorgsky's piano composition *Pictures at an Exhibition*. Composers sometimes transcribe their own works.

Transposition
To change the pitch in which a piece of music is played or sung. In practice this usually means performing the music in a different KEY from the original. *Transposing Instruments* are those which produce notes at a fixed interval of pitch below or above the notes as they are written in a score. In the case of a so-called B-flat clarinet, for example, the instrument sounds the note B flat when the player is reading note C in the score, and it constantly produces notes one tone lower than those written. Such a situation exists because clarinets, and many other woodwind and brass instruments, were traditionally tuned to one particular key.

Treble
1) The highest range of pitch of a boy's voice; 2) the range of pitch of a particular instrument among a family of instruments, e.g. treble recorder; 3) the name of a clef.

Trill
The best-known type of musical ornamentation, created by the rapid alternative playing or singing of two notes, a whole TONE or SEMITONE apart. Indicated in music by the abbreviation 'tr' and a wavy line.

Trio
Piece for three performers, instrumentalists or singers.

Trope
Name for variations made to the melody or words in medieval plainsong and very early polyphonic singing.

Tutti
Italian for 'all', a term used to describe a passage for full orchestra, or full chorus, after one involving only soloists or a small group of players or singers. In a concerto it may simply mean a passage for the orchestra, whether or not everyone is actually playing, in contrast to a passage for the soloist.

Twelve-Tone Music
Music based not on one of the established major or minor keys, but on a particular sequence using all twelve notes of the CHROMATIC SCALE as they exist within an OCTAVE. Schoenberg was the first to develop this type of SERIAL composition, also called DODECAPHONIC music, and it has had a great influence on the music of this century.

Vamp
Very basic sort of instrumental accompaniment to a song, often by a pianist playing by ear.

Variation Form
More fully a theme and variations, consisting firstly of the theme or melody in question, and then of various musical treatments of it. In the seventeenth and eighteenth centuries, sets of variations often involved little more than different

musical decorations of the theme, but
Beethoven and composers after him
used variation form as an expression
of their finest creative ingenuity. It
has frequently been used as the slow
movement of symphonies, concertos,
string quartets and sonatas, sometimes
also as the basis for the last movements of such works.

Vibrato

Italian 'vibrated', describing a slight
variation in pitch of the sounding of a
note, mainly involving singers and
players of bowed stringed instruments. A little vibrato is attractive to
modern ears (there were times in the
past when it was not encouraged),
but too much becomes a wobble.

Virtuoso

A performer, usually referring to an
instrumentalist, of exceptional technical skill. The term can apply also to
music specially associated with
demonstrations of such skill.

Vivace

Italian term of mood or expression,
meaning 'lively'.

Voluntary

Usually an organ piece played at the
beginning or end of church services,
sometimes played from music, sometimes improvized.

Waltz

Dance form with three steady but
lilting beats to the bar, possibly the
most popular of all dances;
occasionally used as a movement
in a symphony, e.g. by Berlioz
and Tchaikovsky.

A fascinating example of how staff notation has developed during this century, taken
from the score of *Circles* by the Italian composer Luciano Berio (born 1925). The work
is for soprano, harp and percussion, and requires the soloist to clap her hands and move
about the concert platform as well as sing.

Acknowledgements

The author wishes to acknowledge the information and useful reference material which he found in the following works:

Big Band Jazz, Albert McCarty (Barrie and Jenkins); *The Bodley Head History of Western Music*, Christopher Headington; *A Concise History of Music*, Percy M. Young (Benn); *Concise Oxford Dictionary of Music*, Percy A. Scholes; *Kobbes Complete Opera Book*, Ed. The Earl of Harewood (Putnam); *Lives of the Great Composers*, Harold Schonberg (Davis-Poynter); *Man and His Music*, Alec Harman and Wilfred Mellers (Barrie and Jenkins); *Music at Court*, Christopher Hogwood (Folio Society); *Music Since the First World War*, Arnold Whittall (Dent); *New Penguin Dictionary of Music*, Arthur Jacob; *Old Musical Instruments*, Rene Clemeuric (Weidenfeld and Nicolson); *A Plain Man's Guide to Jazz*, John Postgate (Honour Books Ltd.).

The author and publishers would like to thank the following for kindly supplying photographs:

Eric Auerbach 73*t*, 80*r*, 83*r*, 84, 90, 91*l*, 101, 105*r*; BBC 61; Ceylon Tourist Board 103; Keith Cheerman/Schott 109; Electronic Music Studios (London) Ltd 63; EMI Records Ltd 11, 79*l*; Fiji Visitors' Bureau 104*t*; Girl Guides Association 10, 26*l*, 30 (Chris Booth), 32*bl*, 51; Houston Rogers 69, 102*l*; Jamaica Tourist Board 15, 29*r*, 52, 104*b*; Jazz Journal 14, 28, 29*l* (Bernard Long), 31; Jazz Music Books, London 66, 113; London Features International 62, 122*r*; Colin Maher 38; Mansell Collection, London 70*r*; National Gallery, London 2, 17, 22, 85, back cover; National Portrait Gallery, London 20, 74*r*, 76*r*, 86*t*, 94*r*, 96*r*, 111, 114; National Youth Orchestra of Great Britain (Lloyds Bank Limited and John Stone) 32*t*; Penguin Books Ltd, Walker & Co., New York 40*r*; Popperfoto 65*l*, 65*r*, 74*l*, 79*l*, 95, 105*l*, 115; Royal College of Music, London 9, 12, 13, 16, 18*l*, 18*r*, 19*l*, 19*r*, 21, 23, 25*r*, 26*tl*, 26*tr*, 70*l*, 71, 72, 73*b*, 76*l*, 77*l*, 77*r*, 78, 80*l*, 83*l*, 87, 88, 93*l*, 93*r*, 94*l*, 97*t*, 97*b*, 98, 99, 100*t*, 100*b*, 102*r*, 106*l*, 106*r*, 107*l*, 107*r*, 108, 110; Royal National Institute for the Blind 25*t*; Royal Opera House, London 89, 96*l*; G. Schirmer Ltd 67; Steinway & Co., 57; Theatre Museum London/Crown Copyright 42*b*, 75, 86*b*, 91*r*, 92, 112; Victoria and Albert Museum London/Crown Copyright 33, 34, 36, 37*l*, 39, 40*l*, 41*l*, 41*r*, 42*t*, 43*l*, 43*r*, 44*l*, 44*r*, 45, 46, 47*l*, 47*r*, 48*l*, 48*r*, 49, 50, 53*l*, 53*r*, 55*t*, 55*b*, 56; Ward Lock Limited 58, 81.

Index

Page numbers in *italics* refer to an illustration